3 2/00
4 8/10

The Poems of Richard Wilbur

3
2/00
6 - 9/10

Young
Adult

BY RICHARD WILBUR

The Beautiful Changes and Other Poems

Ceremony and Other Poems

A Bestiary (editor, with Alexander Calder)

Molière's *The Misanthrope* (translator)

Things of This World

Poems 1943-1958

Candide (with Lillian Hellman)

Poe: Complete Poems (editor)

Advice to a Prophet and Other Poems

Molière's *Tartuffe* (translator)

The Poems of Richard Wilbur

Loudmouse (for children)

Shakespeare: Poems (co-editor, with Alfred Harbage)

Walking to Sleep: New Poems and Translations

Moliére's *The School for Wives* (translator)

Opposites (for children and others)

The Mind-Reader: New Poems

Responses: Prose Pieces: 1953-1976

Moliére's *The Learned Ladies* (translator)

Seven Poems

The Whale & Other Uncollected Translations

Moliére: Four Comedies (translator)

Racine's *Andromache* (translator)

Racine's *Phaedra* (translator)

The Poems of Richard Wilbur

A Harvest/HBJ Book
Harcourt Brace Jovanovich, Publishers
San Diego   New York   London

Requests for permissions to make copies of any part of the work should be mailed to: Permissions, Harcourt Brace Jovanovich, Publishers, Orlando, Florida 32887.

"Beasts," "A Prayer to Go to Paradise with the Donkeys," and "The Pelican" appeared in *A Bestiary*, by Richard Wilbur, copyright, 1955, by Pantheon Books, Inc.

The poems "Grasse: The Olive Trees," "Year's End," "Juggler," "Clearness," "The Sirens," "In the Elegy Season," "Boy at the Window," "The Beacon," "Exeunt" (originally published under the title "Exodus"), "Merlin Enthralled," "After the Last Bulletins," "A Black November Turkey," "All These Birds," "A Baroque Wall-Fountain in the Villa Sciarra," Loves of the Puppets," "Two Voices in a Meadow," "Someone Talking to Himself," "A Fire-Truck," "Advice to a Prophet," "A Grasshopper," "Two Quatrains for First Frost," "In the Smoking-Car," "A Summer Morning," "October Maples, Portland," "Stop," "Ballade for the Duke of Orléans," "Next Door," "The Undead," "A Hole in the Floor," and "The Aspen and the Stream" appeared originally in *The New Yorker*. Other poems appeared originally in *Accent, American Letters, The American Scholar, Atlantic Monthly, Audience, Beloit Poetry Journal, Between Worlds, Botteghe Oscure, Chicago Choice, Foreground, Furioso, Harvard Advocate, Hopkins Review, Hudson Review, Imagi, Inventario, Junior Bazaar, Kenyon Review, Mandrake, The Nation, New Directions No. 10, Nimbus, Origin, Paris Review, Partisan Review, Poetry, Poetry New York, Poetry Quarterly* (London), *Quagga, Quarterly Review of Literature,* Trinity College *Review, Spectrum, Tiger's Eye, Transatlantic Review, Virginia Quarterly,* and *Wake*.

Library of Congress Cataloging in Publication Data
ISBN 0-15-672251-8
Printed in the United States of America

O P Q R

CONTENTS

Things of This World (1956)

Ceremony (1950)

The Beautiful Changes (1947)

Advice to a Prophet

and Other Poems

1961

FOR LILLIAN HELLMAN

A Milkweed

Anonymous as cherubs
Over the crib of God,
White seeds are floating
Out of my burst pod.
What power had I
Before I learned to yield?
Shatter me, great wind:
I shall possess the field.

A Stone

As casual as cow-dung
Under the crib of God,
I lie where chance would have me,
Up to the ears in sod.
Why should I move? To move
Befits a light desire.
The sill of Heaven would founder,
Did such as I aspire.

When you come, as you soon must, to the streets of our city,
Mad-eyed from stating the obvious,
Not proclaiming our fall but begging us
In God's name to have self-pity,

Spare us all word of the weapons, their force and range,
The long numbers that rocket the mind;
Our slow, unreckoning hearts will be left behind,
Unable to fear what is too strange.

Nor shall you scare us with talk of the death of the race.
How should we dream of this place without us?—
The sun mere fire, the leaves untroubled about us,
A stone look on the stone's face?

Speak of the world's own change. Though we cannot conceive
Of an undreamt thing, we know to our cost
How the dreamt cloud crumbles, the vines are blackened
      by frost,
How the view alters. We could believe,

If you told us so, that the white-tailed deer will slip
Into perfect shade, grown perfectly shy,
The lark avoid the reaches of our eye,
The jack-pine lose its knuckled grip

On the cold ledge, and every torrent burn
As Xanthus once, its gliding trout
Stunned in a twinkling. What should we be without
The dolphin's arc, the dove's return,

These things in which we have seen ourselves and spoken?
Ask us, prophet, how we shall call
Our natures forth when that live tongue is all
Dispelled, that glass obscured or broken

In which we have said the rose of our love and the clean
Horse of our courage, in which beheld
The singing locust of the soul unshelled,
And all we mean or wish to mean.

Ask us, ask us whether with the worldless rose
Our hearts shall fail us; come demanding
Whether there shall be lofty or long standing
When the bronze annals of the oak-tree close.

STOP

In grimy winter dusk
We slowed for a concrete platform;
The pillars passed more slowly;
A paper bag leapt up.

The train banged to a standstill.
Brake-steam rose and parted.
Three chipped-at blocks of ice
Sprawled on a baggage-truck.

Out in that glum, cold air
The broken ice lay glintless,
But the truck was painted blue
On side, wheels, and tongue,

A purple, glowering blue
Like the phosphorus of Lethe
Or Queen Persephone's gaze
In the numb fields of the dark.

JUNK

Huru Welandes
　　　　　worc ne geswiceð
monna ænigum
　　　　　ðara ðe Mimming can
heardne gehealdan.

WALDERE

An axe angles
　　　　　　from my neighbor's ashcan;
It is hell's handiwork,
　　　　　　the wood not hickory,
The flow of the grain
　　　　　　not faithfully followed.
The shivered shaft
　　　　　　rises from a shellheap
Of plastic playthings,
　　　　　　paper plates,
And the sheer shards
　　　　　　of shattered tumblers
That were not annealed
　　　　　　for the time needful.
At the same curbside,
　　　　　　a cast-off cabinet
Of wavily-warped
　　　　　　unseasoned wood
Waits to be trundled
　　　　　　in the trash-man's truck.

Haul them off! Hide them!

                        The heart winces
For junk and gimcrack,
                        for jerrybuilt things
And the men who make them
                        for a little money,
Bartering pride
                     like the bought boxer
Who pulls his punches,
                        or the paid-off jockey
Who in the home stretch
                        holds in his horse.
Yet the things themselves
                        in thoughtless honor
Have kept composure,
                        like captives who would not
Talk under torture.
                     Tossed from a tailgate
Where the dump displays
                        its random dolmens,
Its black barrows
                     and blazing valleys,
They shall waste in the weather
                           toward what they were.
The sun shall glory
                     in the glitter of glass-chips,
Foreseeing the salvage
                        of the prisoned sand,
And the blistering paint
                        peel off in patches,
That the good grain
                     be discovered again.

Then burnt, bulldozed,

                                  they shall all be buried

To the depth of diamonds,

                                  in the making dark

Where halt Hephaestus

                                keeps his hammer

And Wayland's work

                            is worn away.

LOVES OF THE PUPPETS

Meeting when all the world was in the bud,
Drawn each to each by instinct's wooden face,
These lovers, heedful of the mystic blood,
Fell glassy-eyed into a hot embrace.

April, unready to be so intense,
Marked time while these outstripped the gentle weather.
Yielded their natures to insensate sense,
And flew apart the more they came together.

Where did they fly? Why, each through such a storm
As may be conjured in a globe of glass
Drove on the colder as the flesh grew warm,
In breathless haste to be at lust's impasse,

To cross the little bridge and sink to rest
In visions of the snow-occluded house
Where languishes, unfound by any quest,
The perfect, small, asphyxiated spouse.

That blizzard ended, and their eyes grew clear,
And there they lay exhausted yet unsated;
Why did their features run with tear on tear,
Until their looks were individuated?

One peace implies another, and they cried
For want of love as if their souls would crack,
Till, in despair of being satisfied,
They vowed at least to share each other's lack.

Then maladroitly they embraced once more,
And hollow rang to hollow with a sound
That tuned the brooks more sweetly than before,
And made the birds explode for miles around.

A SUMMER MORNING

Her young employers, having got in late
From seeing friends in town
And scraped the right front fender on the gate,
Will not, the cook expects, be coming down.

She makes a quiet breakfast for herself.
The coffee-pot is bright,
The jelly where it should be on the shelf.
She breaks an egg into the morning light,

Then, with the bread-knife lifted, stands and hears
The sweet efficient sounds
Of thrush and catbird, and the snip of shears
Where, in the terraced backward of the grounds,

A gardener works before the heat of day.
He straightens for a view
Of the big house ascending stony-gray
Out of his beds mosaic with the dew.

His young employers having got in late,
He and the cook alone
Receive the morning on their old estate,
Possessing what the owners can but own.

A HOLE IN THE FLOOR

for René Magritte

The carpenter's made a hole
In the parlor floor, and I'm standing
Staring down into it now
At four o'clock in the evening,
As Schliemann stood when his shovel
Knocked on the crowns of Troy.

A clean-cut sawdust sparkles
On the grey, shaggy laths,
And here is a cluster of shavings
From the time when the floor was laid.
They are silvery-gold, the color
Of Hesperian apple-parings.

Kneeling, I look in under
Where the joists go into hiding.
A pure street, faintly littered
With bits and strokes of light,
Enters the long darkness
Where its parallels will meet.

The radiator-pipe
Rises in middle distance
Like a shuttered kiosk, standing
Where the only news is night.
Here it's not painted green,
As it is in the visible world.

For God's sake, what am I after?
Some treasure, or tiny garden?
Or that untrodden place,
The house's very soul,
Where time has stored our footbeats
And the long skein of our voices?

Not these, but the buried strangeness
Which nourishes the known:
That spring from which the floor-lamp
Drinks now a wilder bloom,
Inflaming the damask love-seat
And the whole dangerous room.

Jorge Guillén: THE HORSES

Shaggy and heavily natural, they stand
Immobile under their thick and cumbrous manes,
Pent in a barbed enclosure which contains,
By way of compensation, grazing-land.

Nothing disturbs them now. In slow increase
They fatten like the grass. Doomed to be idle,
To haul no cart or wagon, wear no bridle,
They grow into a vegetable peace.

Soul is the issue of so strict a fate.
They harbor visions in their waking eyes,
And with their quiet ears participate
In heaven's pure serenity, which lies
So near all things—yet from the beasts concealed.
Serene now, superhuman, they crop their field.

Je soutenais l'éclat
de la mort toute pure.
VALÉRY

When that dead-certainty appals my thought,
My future trembles on the road ahead.
There where the light of country fields is caught
In the blind, final precinct of the dead,
A wall takes aim.
                              But what is sad, stripped bare
By the sun's gaze? It does not matter now,—
Not yet. What matters is the ripened pear
That even now my hand strips from the bough.

The time will come: my hand will reach, some day,
Without desire. That saddest day of all,
I shall not weep, but with a proper awe
For the great force impending, I shall say,
Lay on, just destiny. Let the white wall
Impose on me its uncapricious law.

SHE

What was her beauty in our first estate
When Adam's will was whole, and the least thing
Appeared the gift and creature of his king,
How should we guess? Resemblance had to wait

For separation, and in such a place
She so partook of water, light, and trees
As not to look like any one of these.
He woke and gazed into her naked face.

But then she changed, and coming down amid
The flocks of Abel and the fields of Cain,
Clothed in their wish, her Eden graces hid,
A shape of plenty with a mop of grain,

She broke upon the world, in time took on
The look of every labor and its fruits.
Columnar in a robe of pleated lawn
She cupped her patient hand for attributes,

Was radiant captive of the farthest tower
And shed her honor on the fields of war,
Walked in her garden at the evening hour,
Her shadow like a dark ogival door,

Breasted the seas for all the westward ships
And, come to virgin country, changed again—
A moonlike being truest in eclipse,
And subject goddess of the dreams of men.

Tree, temple, valley, prow, gazelle, machine,
More named and nameless than the morning star,
Lovely in every shape, in all unseen,
We dare not wish to find you as you are,

Whose apparition, biding time until
Desire decay and bring the latter age,
Shall flourish in the ruins of our will
And deck the broken stones like saxifrage.

GEMINI

I

Because poor PUER's both unsure and vain,
Those who befriend him suffer his disdain,
While those who snub him gain his deference. .
He loves his enemies, in a certain sense.

II

It is the power of Heaven to withdraw
Which fills PUELLA with religious awe.
She worships the remoteness of a wraith.
If God should die for her, she'd lose her faith.

THE UNDEAD

Even as children they were late sleepers,
Preferring their dreams, even when quick with monsters.
To the world with all its breakable toys,
Its compacts with the dying;

From the stretched arms of withered trees
They turned, fearing contagion of the mortal,
And even under the plums of summer
Drifted like winter moons.

Secret, unfriendly, pale, possessed
Of the one wish, the thirst for mere survival,
They came, as all extremists do
In time, to a sort of grandeur:

Now, to their Balkan battlements
Above the vulgar town of their first lives,
They rise at the moon's rising. Strange
That their utter self-concern

Should, in the end, have left them selfless:
Mirrors fail to perceive them as they float
Through the great hall and up the staircase;
Nor are the cobwebs broken.

Into the pallid night emerging,
Wrapped in their flapping capes, routinely maddened
By a wolf's cry, they stand for a moment
Stoking the mind's eye

With lewd thoughts of the pressed flowers
And bric-a-brac of rooms with something to lose,—
Of love-dismembered dolls, and children
Buried in quilted sleep.

Then they are off in a negative frenzy,
Their black shapes cropped into sudden bats
That swarm, burst, and are gone. Thinking
Of a thrush cold in the leaves

Who has sung his few summers truly,
Or an old scholar resting his eyes at last,
We cannot be much impressed with vampires,
Colorful though they are;

Nevertheless, their pain is real,
And requires our pity. Think how sad it must be
To thirst always for a scorned elixir,
The salt quotidian blood

Which, if mistrusted, has no savor;
To prey on life forever and not possess it,
As rock-hollows, tide after tide,
Glassily strand the sea.

The leaves, though little time they have to live,
Were never so unfallen as today,
And seem to yield us through a rustled sieve
The very light from which time fell away.

A showered fire we thought forever lost
Redeems the air. Where friends in passing meet,
They parley in the tongues of Pentecost.
Gold ranks of temples flank the dazzled street.

It is a light of maples, and will go;
But not before it washes eye and brain
With such a tincture, such a sanguine glow
As cannot fail to leave a lasting stain.

So Mary's laundered mantle (in the tale
Which, like all pretty tales, may still be true),
Spread on the rosemary-bush, so drenched the pale
Slight blooms in its irradiated hue,

They could not choose but to return in blue.

I

Hung from a foot, I walk upon my head,
And leave a trail of headprints where I tread!
Yet many of my kind are thus bestead.

II

I have borne more than a body ought to bear.
Three souls I harbored; when I lost a pair,
The third one all but perished then and there.

III

I bite, when bitten; but because I lack
For teeth, no biter scruples to attack,
And many bite me to be bitten back.

IV

Unequal in degree, alike in size,
We make our flight, ascending toward the skies
And rise with those who by our help can rise.

V

Mine was the strangest birth under the sun;
I left the womb, yet life had not begun;
Entered the world, and yet was seen by none.

VI

Sweet purlings in an earth-walled inn resound.
Within that inn a silent guest is found.
Together, guest and inn are onward bound.

VII

All teeth from head to foot (yet friend to men),
I rip and tear my green-haired prey; but then,
All that I chew I spew right out again.

VIII

To me, and through me, Fortune is unkind.
Though iron-bound, yet many must I bind—
And many free, though I remain confined.

SHAME

It is a cramped little state with no foreign policy,
Save to be thought inoffensive. The grammar of the
    language
Has never been fathomed, owing to the national habit
Of allowing each sentence to trail off in confusion.
Those who have visited Scusi, the capital city,
Report that the railway-route from Schuldig passes
Through country best described as unrelieved.
Sheep are the national product. The faint inscription
Over the city gates may perhaps be rendered,
"I'm afraid you won't find much of interest here."
Census-reports which give the population
As zero are, of course, not to be trusted,
Save as reflecting the natives' flustered insistence
That they do not count, as well as their modest horror
Of letting one's sex be known in so many words.
The uniform grey of the nondescript buildings, the
    absence
Of churches or comfort-stations, have given observers
An odd impression of ostentatious meanness,
And it must be said of the citizens (muttering by
In their ratty sheepskins, shying at cracks in the sidewalk)
That they lack the peace of mind of the truly humble.
The tenor of life is careful, even in the stiff
Unsmiling carelessness of the border-guards
And *douaniers,* who admit, whenever they can,
Not merely the usual carloads of deodorant
But gypsies, g-strings, hasheesh, and contraband pigments.

Their complete negligence is reserved, however,
For the hoped-for invasion, at which time the happy people
(Sniggering, ruddily naked, and shamelessly drunk)
Will stun the foe by their overwhelming submission,
Corrupt the generals, infiltrate the staff,
Usurp the throne, proclaim themselves to be sun-gods,
And bring about the collapse of the whole empire.

A GRASSHOPPER

But for a brief
Moment, a poised minute,
He paused on the chicory-leaf;
Yet within it

The sprung perch
Had time to absorb the shock,
Narrow its pitch and lurch,
Cease to rock.

A quiet spread
Over the neighbor ground;
No flower swayed its head
For yards around;

The wind shrank
Away with a swallowed hiss;
Caught in a widening, blank
Parenthesis,

Cry upon cry
Faltered and faded out;
Everything seemed to die.
Oh, without doubt

Peace like a plague
Had gone to the world's verge,
But that an aimless, vague
Grasshopper-urge

Leapt him aloft,
Giving the leaf a kick,
Starting the grasses' soft
Chafe and tick,

So that the sleeping
Crickets resumed their chimes,
And all things wakened, keeping
Their several times.

In gay release
The whole field did what it did,
Peaceful now that its peace
Lay busily hid.

Salvatore Quasimodo:

THE AGRIGENTUM ROAD

That wind's still there that I remember afire
In the manes of the racing horses
Veering across the plains; a wind
That stains the sandstone and erodes the hearts
Of downed columnar statues in the grass.
Oh antique soul, bled white
By rancor, back you lean to that wind again,
Catching the delicate fetor of the moss
That clothes those giants tumbled down by heaven.
How lonely it will be, the time that is left you!
    Worse, worse, if you should hear
That sound again, borne toward the far-off sea
Which Hesperus already pinks with morning:
The jew's-harp quavering sadly in the mouth
Of the wagon-maker climbing
Slowly his moon-washed hill, amidst
The murmur of the Saracen olive trees.

The Aspen

Beholding element, in whose pure eye
My boughs upon a ground of heaven lie—
O deep surrendered mind, where cloud and stone
Compose their beings and efface your own,
Teach me, like you, to drink creation whole
And, casting out my self, become a soul.

The Stream

Why should the water drink,
Blithering little tree?
Think what you choose to think,
But lisp no more at me.

I seek an empty mind.
Reflection is my curse.
Oh, never have I been blind
To the damned universe,

Save when I rose in flood
And in my lathered flight
So fouled myself with mud
As to be purged of sight.

The Aspen

Your water livens me, but not your word,
If what you spoke was what I thought I heard.
But likely I mistook you. What with the claims
Of crow and cricket teaching me their names,
And all this flap and shifting in my head,
I must have lost the drift of what you said.

The Stream

There may be rocks ahead
Where, shivered into smoke
And brawling in my bed,
I'll shred this gaudy cloak;

Then, dodging down a trough
Into a rocky hole,
I'll shake the daylight off
And repossess my soul

In blackness and in fall,
Where self to self shall roar
Till, deaf and blind to all,
I shall be self no more.

The Aspen

Out of your sullen flux I shall distil
A gayer spirit and a clambering will,
And reach toward all about me, and ensnare
With roots the earth, with branches all the air—
Even if that blind groping but achieves
A darker head, a few more aspen-leaves.

A FIRE-TRUCK

Right down the shocked street with a siren-blast
That sends all else skittering to the curb,
Redness, brass, ladders and hats hurl past,
    Blurring to sheer verb,

Shift at the corner into uproarious gear
And make it around the turn in a squall of traction,
The headlong bell maintaining sure and clear,
    Thought is degraded action!

Beautiful, heavy, unweary, loud, obvious thing!
I stand here purged of nuance, my mind a blank.
All I was brooding upon has taken wing,
    And I have you to thank.

As you howl beyond hearing I carry you into my mind,
Ladders and brass and all, there to admire
Your phoenix-red simplicity, enshrined
    In that not extinguished fire.

Even when first her face,
Younger than any spring,
Older than Pharaoh's grain
And fresh as Phoenix-ashes,
Shadowed under its lashes
Every earthly thing,
There was another place
I saw in a flash of pain:
Off in the fathomless dark
Beyond the verge of love
I saw blind fishes move,
And under a stone shelf
Rode the recusant shark—
Cold, waiting, himself.

Oh, even when we fell,
Clean as a mountain source
And barely able to tell
Such ecstasy from grace,
Into the primal bed
And current of our race,
We knew yet must deny
To what we gathered head:
That music growing harsh,
Trees blotting the sky
Above the roaring course
That in the summer's drought
Slowly would peter out
Into a dry marsh.

Love is the greatest mercy
A volley of the sun
That lashes all with shade,
That the first day be mended;
And yet, so soon undone,
It is the lover's curse
Till time be comprehended
And the flawed heart unmade.
What can I do but move
From folly to defeat,
And call that sorrow sweet
That teaches us to see
The final face of love
In what we cannot be?

The eyelids meet. He'll catch a little nap.
The grizzled, crew-cut head drops to his chest.
It shakes above the briefcase on his lap.
Close voices breathe, "Poor sweet, he did his best."

"Poor sweet, poor sweet," the bird-hushed glades repeat,
Through which in quiet pomp his litter goes,
Carried by native girls with naked feet.
A sighing stream concurs in his repose.

Could he but think, he might recall to mind
The righteous mutiny or sudden gale
That beached him here; the dear ones left behind . . .
So near the ending, he forgets the tale.

Were he to lift his eyelids now, he might
Behold his maiden porters, brown and bare.
But even here he has no appetite.
It is enough to know that they are there.

Enough that now a honeyed music swells,
The gentle, mossed declivities begin,
And the whole air is full of flower-smells.
Failure, the longed-for valley, takes him in.

BALLADE FOR THE
DUKE OF ORLÉANS

*who offered a prize at Blois, circa 1457, for
the best ballade employing the line "Je
meurs de soif auprès de la fontaine."*

Flailed from the heart of water in a bow,
He took the falling fly; my line went taut;
Foam was in uproar where he drove below;
In spangling air I fought him and was fought.
Then, wearied to the shallows, he was caught,
Gasped in the net, lay still and stony-eyed.
It was no fading iris I had sought.
I die of thirst, here at the fountain-side.

Down in the harbor's flow and counter-flow
I left my ships with hopes and heroes fraught.
Ten times more golden than the sun could show,
Calypso gave the darkness I besought.
Oh, but her fleecy touch was dearly bought:
All spent, I wakened by my only bride,
Beside whom every vision is but nought,
And die of thirst, here at the fountain-side.

Where does that Plenty dwell, I'd like to know,
Which fathered poor Desire, as Plato taught?
Out on the real and endless waters go
Conquistador and stubborn Argonaut.
Where Buddha bathed, the golden bowl he brought
Gilded the stream, but stalled its living tide.
The sunlight withers as the verse is wrought.
I die of thirst, here at the fountain-side.

Duke, keep your coin. All men are born distraught,
And will not for the world be satisfied.
Whether we live in fact, or but in thought,
We die of thirst, here at the fountain-side.

Gérard de Nerval: *ANTEROS*

You ask me why I bear such rage in heart,
And on this pliant neck a rebel head;
Of great Antaeus' lineage was I bred;
I hurl to heaven again the Victor's dart.

Yea, I am one the Avenger God inspires;
He has marked my forehead with the breath of spite;
My face, like Abel's bloody—alas!—and white,
Burns red by turns with Cain's unsated fires!

The last, Jehovah! who by thy powers fell
And cried against thy tyranny from hell
Was Bel my grandsire, or my father Dagon.

By them thrice baptized in Cocytus' water,
I guard alone the Amalekite my mother,
And sow at her feet the teeth of the old dragon.

TO ISHTAR

Is it less than your brilliance, Ishtar,
How the snowfield smarts in the fresh sun,
And the bells of its melting ring, and we blink
    At the light flexing in trickles?

It is the Spring's disgrace
That already, before the prone arbutus
Will risk its whiteness, you have come down
    To the first gate and darkened.

Forgive us, who cannot conceive you
Elsewhere and maiden, but love you only
Fallen among us in rut and furrow,
    In the shade of amassing leaves,

Or scrawny in plucked harvest,
Your losses having fattened the world
Till crownless, starless, you stoop and enter
    The low door of Irkalla.

There too, in the year's dungeon
Where love takes you, even our itch
For defilement cannot find you out,
    Your death being so perfect.

It is all we can do to witness
The waste motions of empty trees,
The joyless tittering duff, the grass-mats
    Blanched and scurfy with ice,

And in the desert heat
Of vision force from rotten sticks
Those pure and inconceivable blooms
    Which, rising, you bear beyond us.

I

Dear boy, you will not hear me speak
    With sorrow or with rancor
Of what has paled my rosy cheek
    And blasted it with canker;
'Twas Love, great Love, that did the deed
    Through Nature's gentle laws,
And how should ill effects proceed
    From so divine a cause?

Sweet honey comes from bees that sting,
    As you are well aware;
To one adept in reasoning,
Whatever pains disease may bring
Are but the tangy seasoning
    To Love's delicious fare.

II

Columbus and his men, they say,
    Conveyed the virus hither
Whereby my features rot away
    And vital powers wither;
Yet had they not traversed the seas
    And come infected back,

Why, think of all the luxuries
   That modern life would lack!

All bitter things conduce to sweet,
   As this example shows;
Without the little spirochete
We'd have no chocolate to eat,
Nor would tobacco's fragrance greet
   The European nose.

III

Each nation guards its native land
   With cannon and with sentry,
Inspectors look for contraband
   At every port of entry,
Yet nothing can prevent the spread
   Of Love's divine disease:
It rounds the world from bed to bed
   As pretty as you please.

Men worship Venus everywhere,
   As plainly may be seen;
The decorations which I bear
Are nobler than the Croix de Guerre,
And gained in service of our fair
   And universal Queen.

TWO QUATRAINS FOR FIRST FROST

I

Hot summer has exhausted her intent
To the last rose and roundelay and seed.
No leaf has changed, and yet these leaves now read
Like a love-letter that's no longer meant.

II

Now on all things is the dull restive mood
Of some rich gambler who in quick disdain
Plumps all on zero, hoping so to gain
Fresh air, light pockets, and his solitude.

ANOTHER VOICE

The sword bites for peace,
Yet how should that be said
Now or in howling Greece
Above the sorry dead?
Corcyra! cry the crows,
And blacken all our sky.
The soul knows what it knows,
But may not make reply.

From a good face gone mad,
From false or hissing tongue,
What comfort's to be had,
What sweetness can be wrung?
It is the human thing
To reckon pain as pain.
If soul in quiet sing,
Better not to explain.

Great martyrs mocked their pain
And sang that wrong was right;
Great doctors proved them sane
By logic's drier light;
Yet in those I love the most
Some anger, love, or tact
Hushes the giddy ghost
Before atrocious fact.

Forgive me, patient voice
Whose word I little doubt,
Who stubbornly rejoice
When all but beaten out,
If I equivocate,
And will not yet unlearn
Anxiety and hate,
Sorrow and dear concern.

ORGON, CLÉANTE, DORINE

ORGON
Ah, Brother, good-day.

CLÉANTE
Well, welcome back. I'm sorry I can't stay.
How was the country? Blooming, I trust, and green?

ORGON
Excuse me, Brother; just one moment. (*to Dorine:*) Dorine . . .
(*to Cléante:*)
To put my mind at rest, I always learn
The household news the moment I return.
(*to Dorine:*)
Has all been well, these two days I've been gone?
How are the family? What's been going on?

DORINE
Your wife, two days ago, had a bad fever,
And a fierce headache that refused to leave her.

ORGON
Ah. And Tartuffe?

DORINE
Tartuffe? Why, he's round and red,
Bursting with health, and excellently fed.

ORGON
Poor devil!

DORINE

That night, the mistress was unable
To take a single bite at the dinner-table.
Her headache-pains, she said, were simply hellish.

ORGON

Ah. And Tartuffe?

DORINE

He ate his meal with relish,
And zealously devoured in her presence
A leg of mutton and a brace of pheasants.

ORGON

Poor devil!

DORINE

Well, the pains continued strong,
And so she tossed and tossed the whole night long,—
Now icy-cold, now burning like a flame.
We sat beside her bed till morning came.

ORGON

Ah. And Tartuffe?

DORINE

Why, having eaten, he rose
And sought his room, already in a doze,
Got into his warm bed, and snored away
In perfect peace until the break of day.

ORGON

Poor devil!

After much ado, we talked her
Into dispatching someone for the doctor.
He bled her, and the fever quickly fell.

ORGON

Ah. And Tartuffe?

DORINE

He bore it very well.
To keep his cheerfulness at any cost,
And make up for the blood *Madame* had lost,
He drank, at lunch, four beakers full of port.

ORGON

Poor devil!

DORINE

Both are much improved, in short.
I'll go and tell *Madame* that you've expressed
Keen sympathy and anxious interest.

FALL IN CORRALES

Winter will be feasts and fires in the shut houses,
Lovers with hot mouths in their blanched bed,
Prayers and poems made, and all recourses
Against the world huge and dead:

Charms, all charms, as in stillness of plumb summer
The shut head lies down in bottomless grasses,
Willing that its thought be all heat and hum,
That it not dream the time passes.

Now as these light buildings of summer begin
To crumble, the air husky with blown tile,
It is as when in bald April the wind
Unhoused the spirit for a while:

Then there was no need by tales or drowsing
To make the thing that we were mothered by;
It was ourselves who melted in the mountains,
And the sun dove into every eye.

Our desires dwelt in the weather as fine as bomb-dust;
It was our sex that made the fountains yield;
Our flesh fought in the roots, and at last rested
Whole among cows in the risen field.

Now in its empty bed the truant river
Leaves but the perfect rumples of its flow;
The cottonwoods are spending gold like water;
Weeds in their light detachments go;

In a dry world more huge than rhyme or dreaming
We hear the sentences of straws and stones,
Stand in the wind and, bowing to this time,
Practise the candor of our bones.

The home for the aged opens its windows in May,
    And the stale voices of winter-long
Flap from their dusty curtains toward our wood,
    That now with robin-song

Rouses, and is regaled. Promptly the trees
    Break bud and startle into leaf,
Blotting the old from sight, while all the birds
    Repeal the winter's grief

Pitilessly, resolving every sigh
    Or quaver to a chipper trill,
And snaring the sick cough within the rapt
    Beat of the flicker's bill.

Must we not see or hear these worn and frail?
    They are such hearts, for all we know,
As will not cheat the world of their regard,
    Even as they let it go.

Seated, perhaps, along a shady porch
    In the calm, wicker stalls of age,
Old crones and played-out cronies, they project
    Upon a cloudy stage

Gossip of strong-man, dancer, priest, and all
    They knew who had the gift of life,
Artisan, lover, soldier, orator,
    Wild bitch and happy wife,

Lying the more as recollection fails,
  Until for their enchanted souls
The players are forgotten, and they see
    Only such naked rôles

As David was, or Helen, and invent
  Out of their fabulous memories
Alcestis climbing home again, with big
    Death-bullying Heracles.

Is it like this? We have no way to know.
  Our lawn is loud with girls and boys.
The leaves are full and busy with the sun.
    The birds make too much noise.

A CHRISTMAS HYMN

And some of the Pharisees from among the multitude said unto him, Master, rebuke thy disciples.

And he answered and said unto them, I tell you that, if these should hold their peace, the stones would immediately cry out.
ST. LUKE XIX, 39-40

A stable-lamp is lighted
Whose glow shall wake the sky;
The stars shall bend their voices,
And every stone shall cry.
And every stone shall cry,
And straw like gold shall shine;
A barn shall harbor heaven,
A stall become a shrine.

This child through David's city
Shall ride in triumph by;
The palm shall strew its branches,
And every stone shall cry.
And every stone shall cry,
Though heavy, dull, and dumb,
And lie within the roadway
To pave his kingdom come.

Yet he shall be forsaken,
And yielded up to die;
The sky shall groan and darken,
And every stone shall cry.
And every stone shall cry
For stony hearts of men:
God's blood upon the spearhead,
God's love refused again.

But now, as at the ending,
The low is lifted high;
The stars shall bend their voices,
And every stone shall cry.
And every stone shall cry
In praises of the child
By whose descent among us
The worlds are reconciled.

NOTES

ADVICE TO A PROPHET: Hephaestus, invoked by Achilles, scalded the river Xanthus (Scamander) in *Iliad,* xxi.

JUNK: The epigraph, taken from a fragmentary Anglo-Saxon poem, concerns the legendary smith Wayland, and may roughly be translated: "Truly, Wayland's handiwork—the sword Mimming which he made—will never fail any man who knows how to use it bravely."

THE UNDEAD: The *Standard Dictionary of Folklore, Mythology, and Legend* defines the vampire as "One of the types of the undead; a living corpse or soulless body that comes from its burial place and drinks the blood of the living."

EIGHT RIDDLES FROM SYMPHOSIUS: The answers to these riddles of Symphosius (A.D. Fourth Century?) are as follows: I, hobnail; II, mother of twins; III, onion; IV, stairs; V, chick in the egg; VI, river and fish; VII, saw; VIII, chain or fetter.

A FIRE TRUCK: Line 8 echoes a notion entertained by Henry Adams in his "Letter to American Teachers of History" (1910).

Things of This World

1956

FOR
ELLEN,
CHRISTOPHER,
AND
NATHAN

ALTITUDES

I

Look up into the dome:
It is a great salon, a brilliant place,
    Yet not too splendid for the race
Whom we imagine there, wholly at home

    With the gold-rosetted white
Wainscot, the oval windows, and the fault-
    Less figures of the painted vault.
Strolling, conversing in that precious light,

    They chat no doubt of love,
The pleasant burden of their courtesy
    Borne down at times to you and me
Where, in this dark, we stand and gaze above.

    For all they cannot share,
All that the world cannot in fact afford,
    Their lofty premises are floored
With the massed voices of continual prayer.

II

    How far it is from here
To Emily Dickinson's father's house in America;
    Think of her climbing a spiral stair
Up to the little cupola with its clear

    Small panes, its room for one.
Like the dark house below, so full of eyes
    In mirrors and of shut-in flies,
This chamber furnished only with the sun

Is she and she alone,
A mood to which she rises, in which she sees
    Bird-choristers in all the trees
And a wild shining of the pure unknown

    On Amherst. This is caught
In the dormers of a neighbor, who, no doubt,
    Will before long be coming out
To pace about his garden, lost in thought.

LOVE CALLS US TO THE THINGS
OF THIS WORLD

The eyes open to a cry of pulleys,
And spirited from sleep, the astounded soul
Hangs for a moment bodiless and simple
As false dawn.
                Outside the open window
The morning air is all awash with angels.

    Some are in bed-sheets, some are in blouses,
Some are in smocks: but truly there they are.
Now they are rising together in calm swells
Of halcyon feeling, filling whatever they wear
With the deep joy of their impersonal breathing;

    Now they are flying in place, conveying
The terrible speed of their omnipresence, moving
And staying like white water; and now of a sudden
They swoon down into so rapt a quiet
That nobody seems to be there.
                    The soul shrinks

    From all that it is about to remember,
From the punctual rape of every blessèd day,
And cries,
          "Oh, let there be nothing on earth but laundry,
Nothing but rosy hands in the rising steam
And clear dances done in the sight of heaven."

    Yet, as the sun acknowledges
With a warm look the world's hunks and colors,
The soul descends once more in bitter love
To accept the waking body, saying now
In a changed voice as the man yawns and rises,

"Bring them down from their ruddy gallows;
Let there be clean linen for the backs of thieves;
Let lovers go fresh and sweet to be undone,
And the heaviest nuns walk in a pure floating
Of dark habits,
                    keeping their difficult balance.'

SONNET

The winter deepening, the hay all in,
The barn fat with cattle, the apple-crop
Conveyed to market or the fragrant bin,
He thinks the time has come to make a stop,

And sinks half-grudging in his firelit seat,
Though with his heavy body's full consent,
In what would be the posture of defeat,
But for that look of rigorous content.

Outside, the night dives down like one great crow
Against his cast-off clothing where it stands
Up to the knees in miles of hustled snow,

Flapping and jumping like a kind of fire,
And floating skyward its abandoned hands
In gestures of invincible desire.

PIAZZA DI SPAGNA,
EARLY MORNING

I can't forget
How she stood at the top of that long marble stair
Amazed, and then with a sleepy pirouette
Went dancing slowly down to the fountain-quieted square;

Nothing upon her face
But some impersonal loneliness,—not then a girl,
But as it were a reverie of the place,
A called-for falling glide and whirl;

As when a leaf, petal, or thin chip
Is drawn to the falls of a pool and, circling a moment above it,
Rides on over the lip—
Perfectly beautiful, perfectly ignorant of it.

JOHN CHRYSOSTOM

He who had gone a beast
Down on his knees and hands
Remembering lust and murder
Felt now a gust of grace,
Lifted his burnished face
From the psalter of the sands
And found his thoughts in order
And cleared his throat at last.

What they heard was a voice
That spoke what they could learn
From any gelded priest,
Yet rang like a great choir,
He having taught hell's fire
A singing way to burn,
And borrowed of some dumb beast
The wildness to rejoice.

A BLACK NOVEMBER TURKEY

to A. M. *and* A. M.

Nine white chickens come
With haunchy walk and heads
Jabbing among the chips, the chaff, the stones
    And the cornhusk-shreds,

And bit by bit infringe
A pond of dusty light,
Spectral in shadow until they bobbingly one
    By one ignite.

Neither pale nor bright,
The turkey-cock parades
Through radiant squalors, darkly auspicious as
    The ace of spades,

Himself his own cortège
And puffed with the pomp of death,
Rehearsing over and over with strangled râle
    His latest breath.

The vast black body floats
Above the crossing knees
As a cloud over thrashed branches, a calm ship
    Over choppy seas,

Shuddering its fan and feathers
In fine soft clashes
With the cold sound that the wind makes, fondling
    Paper-ashes.

The pale-blue bony head
Set on its shepherd's-crook
Like a saint's death-mask, turns a vague, superb
And timeless look

Upon these clocking hens
And the cocks that one by one,
Dawn after mortal dawn, with vulgar joy
Acclaim the sun.

MIND

Mind in its purest play is like some bat
That beats about in caverns all alone,
Contriving by a kind of senseless wit
Not to conclude against a wall of stone.

It has no need to falter or explore;
Darkly it knows what obstacles are there,
And so may weave and flitter, dip and soar
In perfect courses through the blackest air.

And has this simile a like perfection?
The mind is like a bat. Precisely. Save
That in the very happiest intellection
A graceful error may correct the cave.

AFTER THE LAST BULLETINS

After the last bulletins the windows darken
And the whole city founders readily and deep,
Sliding on all its pillows
To the thronged Atlantis of personal sleep,

And the wind rises. The wind rises and bowls
The day's litter of news in the alleys. Trash
Tears itself on the railings,
Soars and falls with a soft crash,

Tumbles and soars again. Unruly flights
Scamper the park, and taking a statue for dead
Strike at the positive eyes,
Batter and flap the stolid head

And scratch the noble name. In empty lots
Our journals spiral in a fierce noyade
Of all we thought to think,
Or caught in corners cramp and wad

And twist our words. And some from gutters flail
Their tatters at the tired patrolman's feet,
Like all that fisted snow
That cried beside his long retreat

Damn you! damn you! to the emperor's horse's heels.
Oh none too soon through the air white and dry
Will the clear announcer's voice
Beat like a dove, and you and I

From the heart's anarch and responsible town
Return by subway-mouth to life again,
Bearing the morning papers,
And cross the park where saintlike men,

White and absorbed, with stick and bag remove
The litter of the night, and footsteps rouse
With confident morning sound
The songbirds in the public boughs.

LAMARCK ELABORATED

"The environment creates the organ"

The Greeks were wrong who said our eyes have rays;
Not from these sockets or these sparkling poles
Comes the illumination of our days.
It was the sun that bored these two blue holes.

It was the song of doves begot the ear
And not the ear that first conceived of sound:
That organ bloomed in vibrant atmosphere,
As music conjured Ilium from the ground.

The yielding water, the repugnant stone,
The poisoned berry and the flaring rose
Attired in sense the tactless finger-bone
And set the taste-buds and inspired the nose.

Out of our vivid ambiance came unsought
All sense but that most formidably dim.
The shell of balance rolls in seas of thought.
It was the mind that taught the head to swim.

Newtonian numbers set to cosmic lyres
Whelmed us in whirling worlds we could not know,
And by the imagined floods of our desires
The voice of Sirens gave us vertigo.

Though the unseen may vanish, though insight fails
And doubter and downcast saint
Join in the same complaint,
What holy things were ever frightened off
By a fly's buzz, or itches, or a cough?
Harder than nails

They are, more warmly constant than the sun,
At whose continual sign
The dimly prompted vine
Upbraids itself to a green excellence.
What evening, when the slow and forced expense
Of sweat is done,

Does not the dark come flooding the straight furrow
Or filling the well-made bowl?
What night will not the whole
Sky with its clear studs and steady spheres
Turn on a sound chimney? It is seventeen years
Come tomorrow

That Bruna Sandoval has kept the church
Of San Ysidro, sweeping
And scrubbing the aisles, keeping
The candlesticks and the plaster faces bright,
And seen no visions but the thing done right
From the clay porch

To the white altar. For love and in all weathers
This is what she has done.
Sometimes the early sun
Shines as she flings the scrubwater out, with a crash
Of grimy rainbows, and the stained suds flash
Like angel-feathers.

MERLIN ENTHRALLED

In a while they rose and went out aimlessly riding,
Leaving their drained cups on the table round.
Merlin, Merlin, their hearts cried, where are you hiding?
In all the world was no unnatural sound.

Mystery watched them riding glade by glade;
They saw it darkle from under leafy brows;
But leaves were all its voice, and squirrels made
An alien fracas in the ancient boughs.

Once by a lake-edge something made them stop.
Yet what they found was the thumping of a frog,
Bugs skating on the shut water-top,
Some hairlike algae bleaching on a log.

Gawen thought for a moment that he heard
A whitethorn breathe *Niniane.* That Siren's daughter
Rose in a fort of dreams and spoke the word
Sleep, her voice like dark diving water;

And Merlin slept, who had imagined her
Of water-sounds and the deep unsoundable swell
A creature to bewitch a sorcerer,
And lay there now within her towering spell.

Slowly the shapes of searching men and horses
Escaped him as he dreamt on that high bed:
History died; he gathered in its forces;
The mists of time condensed in the still head

Until his mind, as clear as mountain water,
Went raveling toward the deep transparent dream

Who bade him sleep. And then the Siren's daughter
Received him as the sea receives a stream.

Fate would be fated; dreams desire to sleep.
This the forsaken will not understand.
Arthur upon the road began to weep
And said to Gawen *Remember when this hand*

Once haled a sword from stone; now no less strong
It cannot dream of such a thing to do.
Their mail grew quainter as they clopped along.
The sky became a still and woven blue.

A VOICE FROM UNDER THE TABLE

to Robert and Jane Brooks

How shall the wine be drunk, or the woman known?
I take this world for better or for worse,
But seeing rose carafes conceive the sun
My thirst conceives a fierier universe:
And then I toast the birds in the burning trees
That chant their holy lucid drunkenness;
I swallowed all the phosphorus of the seas
Before I fell into this low distress.

You upright people all remember how
Love drove you first to the woods, and there you heard
The loose-mouthed wind complaining *Thou* and *Thou;*
My gawky limbs were shuddered by the word.
Most of it since was nothing but charades
To spell that hankering out and make an end,
But the softest hands against my shoulder-blades
Only increased the crying of the wind.

For this the goddess rose from the midland sea
And stood above the famous wine-dark wave,
To ease our drouth with clearer mystery
And be a South to all our flights of love.
And down by the selfsame water I have seen
A blazing girl with skin like polished stone
Splashing until a far-out breast of green
Arose and with a rose contagion shone.

"A myrtle-shoot in hand, she danced; her hair
Cast on her back and shoulders a moving shade."
Was it some hovering light that showed her fair?
Was it of chafing dark that light was made?

Perhaps it was Archilochus' fantasy,
Or that his saying sublimed the thing he said.
All true enough; and true as well that she
Was beautiful, and danced, and is now dead.

Helen was no such high discarnate thought
As men in dry symposia pursue,
But was as bitterly fugitive, not to be caught
By what men's arms in love or fight could do.
Groan in your cell; rape Troy with sword and flame;
The end of thirst exceeds experience.
A devil told me it was all the same
Whether to fail by spirit or by sense.

God keep me a damned fool, nor charitably
Receive me into his shapely resignations.
I am a sort of martyr, as you see,
A horizontal monument to patience.
The calves of waitresses parade about
My helpless head upon this sodden floor.
Well, I am down again, but not yet out.
O sweet frustrations, I shall be back for more.

THE BEACON

Founded on rock and facing the night-fouled sea
A beacon blinks at its own brilliance,
Over and over with cutlass gaze
Solving the Gordian waters,

Making the sea-roads out, and the lounge of the weedy
Meadows, finding the blown hair
As it always has, and the buxom, lavish
Romp of the ocean-daughters.

Then in the flashes of darkness it is all gone,
The flung arms and the hips, meads
And meridians, all; and the dark of the eye
Dives for the black pearl

Of the sea-in-itself. Watching the blinded waves
Compounding their eclipse, we hear their
Booms, rumors and guttural sucks
Warn of the pitchy whirl

At the mind's end. All of the sense of the sea
Is veiled as voices nearly heard
In morning sleep; nor shall we wake
At the sea's heart. Rail

At the deaf unbeatable sea, my soul, and weep
Your Alexandrine tears, but look:
The beacon-blaze unsheathing turns
The face of darkness pale

And now with one grand chop gives clearance to
Our human visions, which assume

The waves again, fresh and the same.
Let us suppose that we

See most of darkness by our plainest light.
It is the Nereid's kick endears
The tossing spray; a sighted ship
Assembles all the sea.

STATUES

These children playing at statues fill
The gardens with their shrillness; in a planned
And planted grove they fling from the swinger's hand
Across the giddy grass and then hold still

In gargoyle attitudes,—as if
All definition were outrageous. Then
They melt in giggles and begin again.
Above their heads the maples with a stiff

Compliance entertain the air
In abrupt gusts, losing the look of trees
In rushed and cloudy metamorphoses,
Their shadows all a brilliant disrepair,

A wash of dodging stars, through which
The children weave and then again undo
Their fickle zodiacs. It is a view
Lively as Ovid's Chaos, and its rich

Uncertainty compels the crowd:
Two nuns regard it with habitual love,
Moving along a path as mountains move
Or seem to move when traversed by a cloud;

The soldier breaks his iron pace;
Linked lovers pause to gaze; and every rôle
Relents,—until the feet begin to stroll
Or stride again. But settled in disgrace

Upon his bench, one aging bum,
Brought by his long evasion and distress
Into an adamantine shapelessness,
Stares at the image of his kingdom come.

Five soldiers fixed by Mathew Brady's eye
Stand in a land subdued beyond belief.
Belief might lend them life again. I try
Like orphaned Hamlet working up his grief

To see my spellbound fathers in these men
Who, breathless in their amber atmosphere,
Show but the postures men affected then
And the hermit faces of a finished year.

The guns and gear and all are strange until
Beyond the tents I glimpse a file of trees
Verging a road that struggles up a hill.
They're sycamores.
                          The long-abated breeze

Flares in those boughs I know, and hauls the sound
Of guns and a great forest in distress.
Fathers, I know my cause, and we are bound
Beyond that hill to fight at Wilderness.

II. But trick your eyes with Birnam Wood, or think
    How fire-cast shadows of the bankside trees
    Rode on the back of Simois to sink
    In the wide waters. Reflect how history's

    Changes are like the sea's, which mauls and mulls
    Its salvage of the world in shifty waves,
    Shrouding in evergreen the oldest hulls
    And yielding views of its confounded graves

    To the new moon, the sun, or any eye
    That in its shallow shoreward version sees

The pebbles charging with a deathless cry
And carageen memorials of trees.

III. Now, old man of the sea,
   I start to understand:
   The will will find no stillness
   Back in a stilled land.

   The dead give no command
   And shall not find their voice
   Till they be mustered by
   Some present fatal choice.

   Let me now rejoice
   In all impostures, take
   The shape of lion or leopard,
   Boar, or watery snake,

   Or like the comber break,
   Yet in the end stand fast
   And by some fervent fraud
   Father the waiting past,

   Resembling at the last
   The self-established tree
   That draws all waters toward
   Its live formality.

Charles Baudelaire: L'INVITATION AU VOYAGE

My child, my sister,
>   dream
How sweet all things would seem
Were we in that kind land to live together,
>   And there love slow and long,
>   There love and die among
Those scenes that image you, that sumptuous weather.
>   Drowned suns that glimmer there
>   Through cloud-disheveled air
Move me with such a mystery as appears
>   Within those other skies
>   Of your treacherous eyes
When I behold them shining through their tears.

There, there is nothing else but grace and measure,
Richness, quietness, and pleasure.

>   Furniture that wears
>   The lustre of the years
Softly would glow within our glowing chamber,
>   Flowers of rarest bloom
>   Proffering their perfume
Mixed with the vague fragrances of amber;
>   Gold ceilings would there be,
>   Mirrors deep as the sea,
The walls all in an Eastern splendor hung—
>   Nothing but should address
>   The soul's loneliness,
Speaking her sweet and secret native tongue.

There, there is nothing else but grace and measure,
Richness, quietness, and pleasure.

See, sheltered from the swells
There in the still canals
Those drowsy ships that dream of sailing forth;
It is to satisfy
Your least desire, they ply
Hither through all the waters of the earth.
The sun at close of day
Clothes the fields of hay,
Then the canals, at last the town entire
In hyacinth and gold:
Slowly the land is rolled
Sleepward under a sea of gentle fire.

There, there is nothing else but grace and measure,
Richness, quietness, and pleasure.

"Far enough down is China," somebody said.
"Dig deep enough and you might see the sky
As clear as at the bottom of a well.
Except it would be real—a different sky.
Then you could burrow down until you came
To China! Oh, it's nothing like New Jersey.
There's people, trees, and houses, and all that,
But much, much different. Nothing looks the same."

I went and got the trowel out of the shed
And sweated like a coolie all that morning,
Digging a hole beside the lilac-bush,
Down on my hands and knees. It was a sort
Of praying, I suspect. I watched my hand
Dig deep and darker, and I tried and tried
To dream a place where nothing was the same.
The trowel never did break through to blue.

Before the dream could weary of itself
My eyes were tired of looking into darkness,
My sunbaked head of hanging down a hole.
I stood up in a place I had forgotten,
Blinking and staggering while the earth went round
And showed me silver barns, the fields dozing
In palls of brightness, patens growing and gone
In the tides of leaves, and the whole sky china blue.
Until I got my balance back again
All that I saw was China, China, China.

Francis Jammes: A PRAYER TO GO TO PARADISE WITH THE DONKEYS

to Máire and Jack

When I must come to you, O my God, I pray
It be some dusty-roaded holiday,
And even as in my travels here below,
I beg to choose by what road I shall go
To Paradise, where the clear stars shine by day.
I'll take my walking-stick and go my way,
And to my friends the donkeys I shall say,
"I am Francis Jammes, and I'm going to Paradise,
For there is no hell in the land of the loving God."
And I'll say to them: "Come, sweet friends of the blue skies,
Poor creatures who with a flap of the ears or a nod
Of the head shake off the buffets, the bees, the flies . . ."

Let me come with these donkeys, Lord, into your land,
These beasts who bow their heads so gently, and stand
With their small feet joined together in a fashion
Utterly gentle, asking your compassion.
I shall arrive, followed by their thousands of ears,
Followed by those with baskets at their flanks,
By those who lug the carts of mountebanks
Or loads of feather-dusters and kitchen-wares,
By those with humps of battered water-cans,
By bottle-shaped she-asses who halt and stumble,
By those tricked out in little pantaloons
To cover their wet, blue galls where flies assemble
In whirling swarms, making a drunken hum.
Dear God, let it be with these donkeys that I come,
And let it be that angels lead us in peace
To leafy streams where cherries tremble in air,

Sleek as the laughing flesh of girls; and there
In that haven of souls let it be that, leaning above
Your divine waters, I shall resemble these donkeys,
Whose humble and sweet poverty will appear
Clear in the clearness of your eternal love.

PELLICANUS is the word
    For a certain breed of bird
Who truly is a crane;
    Egypt is his domain.
There are two kinds thereof;
    Near to the Nile they live;
One of them dwells in the flood,
    The fishes are his food;
The other lives in the isles
    On lizards, crocodiles,
Serpents, and stinking creatures,
    And beasts of evil nature.
In Greek his title was
    Onocrotalos,
Which is *longum rostrum,* said
    In the Latin tongue instead,
Or *long-beak* in our own.
    Of this bird it is known
That when he comes to his young,
    They being grown and strong,
And does them kindly things,
    And covers them with his wings,
The little birds begin
    Fiercely to peck at him;
They tear at him and try
    To blind their father's eye.
He falls upon them then
    And slays them with great pain,
Then goes away for a spell,
    Leaving them where they fell.
On the third day he returns,
    And thereupon he mourns,

Feeling so strong a woe
    To see the small birds so
That he strikes his breast with his beak
    Until the blood shall leak.
And when the coursing blood
    Spatters his lifeless brood,
Such virtue does it have
    That once again they live.

K N O W that this pelican
    Signifies Mary's Son;
The little birds are men
    Restored to life again
From death, by that dear blood
    Shed for us by our God.
Now learn one meaning more,
    Revealed by holy lore:
Know why the small birds try
    To peck their father's eye,
Who turns on them in wrath
    And puts them all to death.
Men who deny the light
    Would blind God's blazing sight,
But on such people all
    His punishment will fall.
This is the meaning I find;
    Now bear it well in mind.

APOLOGY

A word sticks in the wind's throat;
A wind-launch drifts in the swells of rye;
Sometimes, in broad silence,
The hanging apples distil their darkness.

You, in a green dress, calling, and with brown hair,
Who come by the field-path now, whose name I say
Softly, forgive me love if also I call you
Wind's word, apple-heart, haven of grasses.

It is I, O Azure, come from the caves below
To hear the waves clamber the loudening shores,
And see those barks again in the dawn's glow
Borne out of darkness, swept by golden oars.

My solitary hands call back the lords
Whose salty beards beguiled my finger-tips;
I wept. They sang the prowess of their swords
And what great bays fled sternward of their ships.

I hear the martial trumpets and the deep-
Sea conches cry a cadence to the sweeps;
The oarsmen's chantey holds the storm in sway;

And high on the hero prows the Gods I see,
Their antique smiles insulted by the spray,
Reaching their carved, indulgent arms to me.

Beasts in their major freedom
Slumber in peace tonight. The gull on his ledge
Dreams in the guts of himself the moon-plucked waves below,
    And the sunfish leans on a stone, slept
        By the lyric water,

In which the spotless feet
Of deer make dulcet splashes, and to which
The ripped mouse, safe in the owl's talon, cries
    Concordance. Here there is no such harm
        And no such darkness

As the selfsame moon observes
Where, warped in window-glass, it sponsors now
The werewolf's painful change. Turning his head away
    On the sweaty bolster, he tries to remember
        The mood of manhood,

But lies at last, as always,
Letting it happen, the fierce fur soft to his face,
Hearing with sharper ears the wind's exciting minors,
    The leaves' panic, and the degradation
        Of the heavy streams.

Meantime, at high windows
Far from thicket and pad-fall, suitors of excellence
Sigh and turn from their work to construe again the painful
    Beauty of heaven, the lucid moon
        And the risen hunter,

Making such dreams for men
As told will break their hearts as always, bringing
Monsters into the city, crows on the public statues,
Navies fed to the fish in the dark
Unbridled waters.

EXEUNT

Piecemeal the summer dies;
At the field's edge a daisy lives alone;
A last shawl of burning lies
On a gray field-stone.

All cries are thin and terse;
The field has droned the summer's final mass;
A cricket like a dwindled hearse
Crawls from the dry grass.

Things concentrate at the edges; the pond-surface
Is bourne to fish and man and it is spread
In textile scum and damask light, on which
The lily-pads are set; and there are also
 Inlaid ruddy twigs, becalmed pine-leaves,
 Air-baubles, and the chain mail of froth.

Descending into sleep (as when the night-lift
Falls past a brilliant floor), we glimpse a sublime
Décor and hear, perhaps, a complete music,
But this evades us, as in the night meadows
 The crickets' million roundsong dies away
 From all advances, rising in every distance.

Our riches are centrifugal; men compose
Daily, unwittingly, their final dreams,
And those are our own voices whose remote
Consummate chorus rides on the whirlpool's rim,
 Past which we flog our sails, toward which we drift,
 Plying our trades, in hopes of a good drowning.

BOY AT THE WINDOW

Seeing the snowman standing all alone
In dusk and cold is more than he can bear.
The small boy weeps to hear the wind prepare
A night of gnashings and enormous moan.
His tearful sight can hardly reach to where
The pale-faced figure with bitumen eyes
Returns him such a god-forsaken stare
As outcast Adam gave to Paradise.

The man of snow is, nonetheless, content,
Having no wish to go inside and die.
Still, he is moved to see the youngster cry.
Though frozen water is his element,
He melts enough to drop from one soft eye
A trickle of the purest rain, a tear
For the child at the bright pane surrounded by
Such warmth, such light, such love, and so much fear.

SPEECH FOR THE REPEAL OF THE McCARRAN ACT

As Wulfstan said on another occasion,
The strong net bellies in the wind and the spider rides it out;
But history, that sure blunderer,
Ruins the unkempt web, however silver.

I am not speaking of rose windows
Shattered by bomb-shock; the leads touselled; the glass-grains
    broadcast;
If the rose be living at all
A gay gravel shall be pollen of churches.

Nor do I mean railway networks.
Torn-up tracks are no great trouble. As Wulfstan said,
It is oathbreach, faithbreach, lovebreach
Bring the invaders into the estuaries.

Shall one man drive before him ten
Unstrung from sea to sea? Let thought be free. I speak
Of the spirit's weaving, the neural
Web, the self-true mind, the trusty reflex.

ALL THESE BIRDS

Agreed that all these birds,
Hawk or heavenly lark or heard-of nightingale,
   Perform upon the kitestrings of our sight
   In a false distance, that the day and night
   Are full of wingèd words

                                   gone rather stale,
      That nothing is so worn
      As Philomel's bosom-thorn,

      That it is, in fact, the male
Nightingale which sings, and that all these creatures wear
   Invisible armor such as Hébert beheld
   His water-ousel through, as, wrapped or shelled
   In a clear bellying veil

                        or bubble of air,
      It bucked the flood to feed
      At the stream-bottom. Agreed

      That the sky is a vast claire
In which the gull, despite appearances, is not
   Less claustral than the oyster in its beak
   And dives like nothing human; that we seek
   Vainly to know the heron

                              (but can plot
      What angle of the light
      Provokes its northern flight.)

      Let them be polyglot
And wordless then, those boughs that spoke with Solomon
   In Hebrew canticles, and made him wise;
   And let a clear and bitter wind arise

To storm into the hotbeds
                    of the sun,
     And there, beyond a doubt,
     Batter the Phoenix out.

     Let us, with glass or gun,
Watch (from our clever blinds) the monsters of the sky
     Dwindle to habit, habitat, and song,
     And tell the imagination it is wrong
     Till, lest it be undone,
                    it spin a lie
     So fresh, so pure, so rare
     As to possess the air.

     Why should it be more shy
Than chimney-nesting storks, or sparrows on a wall?
     Oh, let it climb wherever it can cling
     Like some great trumpet-vine, a natural thing
     To which all birds that fly
                         come natural.
     Come, stranger, sister, dove:
     Put on the reins of love.

A BAROQUE WALL-FOUNTAIN
IN THE VILLA SCIARRA

for Dore and Adja

Under the bronze crown
Too big for the head of the stone cherub whose feet
  A serpent has begun to eat,
Sweet water brims a cockle and braids down

    Past spattered mosses, breaks
On the tipped edge of a second shell, and fills
  The massive third below. It spills
In threads then from the scalloped rim, and makes

    A scrim or summery tent
For a faun-ménage and their familiar goose.
  Happ" in all that ragged, loose
Collaps. of water, its effortless descent

    And flatteries of spray,
The stocky god upholds the shell with ease,
  Watching, about his shaggy knees,
The goatish innocence of his babes at play;

    His fauness all the while
Leans forward, slightly, into a clambering mesh
  Of water-lights, her sparkling flesh
In a saecular ecstasy, her blinded smile

    Bent on the sand floor
Of the trefoil pool, where ripple-shadows come
  And go in swift reticulum,
More addling to the eye than wine, and more

Interminable to thought
Than pleasure's calculus. Yet since this all
Is pleasure, flash, and waterfall,
Must it not be too simple? Are we not

More intricately expressed
In the plain fountains that Maderna set
Before St. Peter's—the main jet
Struggling aloft until it seems at rest

In the act of rising, until
The very wish of water is reversed,
That heaviness borne up to burst
In a clear, high, cavorting head, to fill

With blaze, and then in gauze
Delays, in a gnatlike shimmering, in a fine
Illumined version of itself, decline,
And patter on the stones its own applause?

If that is what men are
Or should be, if those water-saints display
The pattern of our areté,*
What of these showered fauns in their bizarre,

Spangled, and plunging house?
They are at rest in fulness of desire
For what is given, they do not tire
Of the smart of the sun, the pleasant water-douse

And riddled pool below,
Reproving our disgust and our ennui

* Note: *areté*, a Greek word meaning roughly "virtue."

With humble insatiety.
Francis, perhaps, who lay in sister snow

    Before the wealthy gate
Freezing and praising, might have seen in this
    No trifle, but a shade of bliss—
That land of tolerable flowers, that state

    As near and far as grass
Where eyes become the sunlight, and the hand
    Is worthy of water: the dreamt land
Toward which all hungers leap, all pleasures pass.

AN EVENT

As if a cast of grain leapt back to the hand,
A landscapeful of small black birds, intent
On the far south, convene at some command
At once in the middle of the air, at once are gone
With headlong and unanimous consent
From the pale trees and fields they settled on.

What is an individual thing? They roll
Like a drunken fingerprint across the sky!
Or so I give their image to my soul
Until, as if refusing to be caught
In any singular vision of my eye
Or in the nets and cages of my thought,

They tower up, shatter, and madden space
With their divergences, are each alone
Swallowed from sight, and leave me in this place
Shaping these images to make them stay:
Meanwhile, in some formation of their own,
They fly me still, and steal my thoughts away.

Delighted with myself and with the birds,
I set them down and give them leave to be.
It is by words and the defeat of words,
Down sudden vistas of the vain attempt,
That for a flying moment one may see
By what cross-purposes the world is dreamt.

A CHRONIC CONDITION

Berkeley did not foresee such misty weather,
Nor centuries of light
Intend so dim a day. Swaddled together
In separateness, the trees
Persist or not beyond the gray-white
Palings of the air. Gone
Are whatever wings bothered the lighted leaves
When leaves there were. Are all
The sparrows fallen? I can hardly hear
My memory of those bees
Which only lately mesmerized the lawn.
Now, something, blaze! A fear
Swaddles me now that Hylas' tree will fall
Where no eye lights and grieves,
Will fall to nothing and without a sound.

I sway and lean above the vanished ground.

THE MILL

The spoiling daylight inched along the bar-top,
Orange and cloudy, slowly igniting lint,
And then that glow was gone, and still your voice,
Serene with failure and with the ease of dying,
Rose from the shades that more and more became you.
Turning among its images, your mind
Produced the names of streets, the exact look
Of lilacs, 1903, in Cincinnati,
—Random, as if your testament were made,
The round sums all bestowed, and now you spent
Your pocket change, so as to be rid of it.
Or was it that you half-hoped to surprise
Your dead life's sound and sovereign anecdote?
What I remember best is the wrecked mill
You stumbled on in Tennessee; or was it
Somewhere down in Brazil? It slips my mind
Already. But there it was in a still valley
Far from the towns. No road or path came near it.
If there had been a clearing now it was gone,
And all you found amidst the choke of green
Was three walls standing, hurdled by great vines
And thatched by height on height of hushing leaves.
But still the mill-wheel turned! its crazy buckets
Creaking and lumbering out of the clogged race
And sounding, as you said, as if you'd found
Time all alone and talking to himself
In his eternal rattle.
                           How should I guess
Where they are gone to, now that you are gone,
Those fading streets and those most fragile lilacs,
Those fragmentary views, those times of day?
All that I can be sure of is the mill-wheel.
It turns and turns in my mind, over and over.

FOR THE NEW RAILWAY STATION
IN ROME

Those who said God is praised
By hurt pillars, who loved to see our brazen lust
    Lie down in rubble, and our vaunting arches
        Conduce to dust;

Those who with short shadows
Poked through the stubbled forum pondering on decline,
    And would not take the sun standing at noon
        For a good sign;

Those pilgrims of defeat
Who brought their injured wills as to a soldiers' home;
    Dig them all up now, tell them there's something new
        To see in Rome.

See, from the travertine
Face of the office block, the roof of the booking-hall
    Sails out into the air beside the ruined
        Servian Wall,

Echoing in its light
And cantilevered swoop of reinforced concrete
    The broken profile of these stones, defeating
        That defeat

And straying the strummed mind,
By such a sudden chord as raised the town of Troy,
    To where the least shard of the world sings out
        In stubborn joy,

"What city is eternal
But that which prints itself within the groping head

Out of the blue unbroken reveries
   Of the building dead?

"What is our praise or pride
But to imagine excellence, and try to make it?
What does it say over the door of Heaven
   But *homo fecit?*"

Ceremony

and Other Poems

1950

TO F.O.M.

THEN

Then when the ample season
Warmed us, waned and went,
We gave to the leaves no graves,
To the robin gone no name,
Nor thought at the birds' return
Of their sourceless dim descent,
And we read no loss in the leaf,
But a freshness ever the same.

The leaf first learned of years
One not forgotten fall;
Of lineage now, and loss
These latter singers tell,
Of a year when birds now still
Were all one choiring call
Till the unreturning leaves
Imperishably fell.

Backtrack of sea, the baywater goes; flats
Bubble in sunlight, running with herringbone streams;
Sea-lettuce lies in oily mats
On sand mislaid; stranded
Are slug, stone, and shell, as dreams
Drain into morning shine, and the cheat is ended.

Oh, it was blue, the too amenable sea.
We heard of pearls in the dark and wished to dive.
But here in this snail-shell see, see
The crab-legs waggle; where,
If altered now, and yet alive,
Did softness get these bitter claws to wear?

As curtains from a fatal window blown
The sea's receding fingers terribly tell
Of strangest things together grown;
All join, and in the furl
Of waters, blind in muck and shell,
Pursue their slow paludal games. O pearl,

Rise, rise and brighten, wear clear air, and in
Your natal cloudiness receive the sun;
Hang among single stars, and twin
My double deep; O tides,
Return a truer blue, make one
The sky's blue speech, and what the sea confides.

"A WORLD WITHOUT OBJECTS
IS A SENSIBLE EMPTINESS"

The tall camels of the spirit
Steer for their deserts, passing the last groves loud
With the sawmill shrill of the locust, to the whole honey
    of the arid
Sun. They are slow, proud,

    And move with a stilted stride
To the land of sheer horizon, hunting Traherne's
Sensible emptiness, there where the brain's lantern-slide
    Revels in vast returns.

    O connoisseurs of thirst,
Beasts of my soul who long to learn to drink
Of pure mirage, those prosperous islands are accurst
    That shimmer on the brink

    Of absence; auras, lustres,
And all shinings need to be shaped and borne.
Think of those painted saints, capped by the early masters
    With bright, jauntily-worn

    Aureate plates, or even
Merry-go-round rings. Turn, O turn
From the fine sleights of the sand, from the long empty oven
    Where flames in flamings burn

    Back to the trees arrayed
In bursts of glare, to the halo-dialing run
Of the country creeks, and the hills' bracken tiaras made
    Gold in the sunken sun,

    Wisely watch for the sight
Of the supernova burgeoning over the barn,
Lampshine blurred in the steam of beasts, the spirit's right
    Oasis, light incarnate.

THE PARDON

My dog lay dead five days without a grave
In the thick of summer, hid in a clump of pine
And a jungle of grass and honeysuckle-vine.
I who had loved him while he kept alive

Went only close enough to where he was
To sniff the heavy honeysuckle-smell
Twined with another odor heavier still
And hear the flies' intolerable buzz.

Well, I was ten and very much afraid.
In my kind world the dead were out of range
And I could not forgive the sad or strange
In beast or man. My father took the spade

And buried him. Last night I saw the grass
Slowly divide (it was the same scene
But now it glowed a fierce and mortal green)
And saw the dog emerging. I confess

I felt afraid again, but still he came
In the carnal sun, clothed in a hymn of flies,
And death was breeding in his lively eyes.
I started in to cry and call his name,

Asking forgiveness of his tongueless head.
. . . I dreamt the past was never past redeeming:
But whether this was false or honest dreaming
I beg death's pardon now. And mourn the dead.

Easy as cove-water rustles its pebbles and shells
In the slosh, spread, seethe, and the backsliding
Wallop and tuck of the wave, and just that cheerful,
    Tables and earth were riding

Back and forth in the minting shades of the trees.
There were whiffs of anise, a clear clinking
Of coins and glasses, a still crepitant sound
    Of the earth in the garden drinking

The late rain. Rousing again, the wind
Was swashing the shadows in relay races
Of sun-spangles over the hands and clothes
    And the drinkers' dazzled faces,

So that when somebody spoke, and asked the question
Comment s'appelle cet arbre-là?
A girl had gold on her tongue, and gave this answer:
    Ça, c'est l'acacia.

POET: The hardest headlands
Gravel down,
The seas abrade
What coasts we know,
And all our maps
In azure drown,
Forewarning us
To rise and go.

And we shall dwell
On the rose of the winds,
Which is the isle
Of every sea,
Surviving there
The tinted lands
Which could not last
Our constancy.

LADY: That roving wave
Where Venus rose
Glints in the floods
Of farthest thought;
What beauty there
In image goes
Dissolves in other
And is not.

There are some shores
Still left to find
Whose broken rocks
Will last the hour;
Forsake those roses
Of the mind
And tend the true,
The mortal flower.

EPISTEMOLOGY

I

Kick at the rock, Sam Johnson, break your bones:
But cloudy, cloudy is the stuff of stones.

II

We milk the cow of the world, and as we do
We whisper in her ear, "You are not true."

I

From blackhearted water colder
Than Cain's blood, and aching with ice, from a gunmetal bay
No one would dream of drowning in, rises
The walrus: head hunched from the oxen shoulder,
The serious face made for surprises
Looks with a thick dismay

At the camera lens which takes
Him in, and takes him back to cities, to volleys of laughter
In film palaces, just as another, brought
By Jonas Poole to England for the sakes
Of James First and his court, was thought
Most strange, and died soon after.

So strangeness gently steels
Us, and curiosity kills, keeping us cool to go
Sail with the hunters unseen to the walrus rock
And stand behind their slaughter: which of us feels
The harpoon's hurt, and the huge shock
When the blood jumps to flow?

Oh, it is hunters alone
Regret the beastly pain, it is they who love the foe
That quarries out their force, and every arrow
Is feathered soft with wishes to atone;
Even the surest sword in sorrow
Bleeds for its spoiling blow.

Sometimes, as one can see
Carved at Amboise in a high relief, on the lintel stone
Of the castle chapel, hunters have strangely come

To a mild close of the chase, bending the knee
  Instead of the bow, struck sweetly dumb
    To see from the brow bone

  Of the hounded stag a cross
Grown, and the eyes clear with grace. Perfectly still
  Are the cruising dogs as well, their paws aground
  In a white hush of lichen. Beds of moss
    Spread, and the clearing wreathes around
      The dear suspense of will.

    But looking higher now
To the chapel steeple, see among points and spines of the
                updrawn
  Vanishing godbound stone, ringing its sped
  Thrust as a target tatters, a round row
    Of real antlers taken from dead
      Deer. The hunt goes on.

                        II

    They built well who made
Those palaces of hunting lords, the grounds planned
  As ruled reaches, always with a view
  Down tapered aisles of trees at last to fade
    In the world's mass. The lords so knew
      Of land beyond their land.

  If, at Versailles, outdrawn
By the stairs or the still canals, by the gradual shrink of an urn
  Or the thousand fountains, a king gave back his gaze
  To the ample balanced windows vantaged on
    The clearness near, and the far haze,
      He learned he must return.

Seen from a palace stair
The wilderness was distance; difference; it spoke
In the strong king's mind for mercy, while to the weak,
To the weary of choice, it told of havens where
The Sabbath stayed, and all were meek,
And justice known a joke.

Some cast their crowns away
And went to live in the distance. There there was nothing
seemed
Remotely strange to them, their innocence
Shone in the special features of the prey
They would not harm. The dread expense
Of golden times they dreamed

Was that their kingdoms fell
The deeper into tyranny, the more they stole
Through Ardens out to Eden isles apart,
Seeking a shore, or shelter of some spell
Where harmlessly the hidden heart
Might hold creation whole.

When to his solitude
The world became as island mists, then Prospero,
Pardoning all, and pardoned, yet aware
The full forgiveness cannot come, renewed
His reign, bidding the boat prepare
From mysteries to go

Toward masteries less sheer,
And Duke again, did rights and mercies, risking wrong,
Found advocates and enemies, and found
His bounded empire good, where he could hear
Below his walls the baying hound
And the loud hunting-song.

MUSEUM PIECE

The good gray guardians of art
Patrol the halls on spongy shoes,
Impartially protective, though
Perhaps suspicious of Toulouse.

Here dozes one against the wall,
Disposed upon a funeral chair.
A Degas dancer pirouettes
Upon the parting of his hair.

See how she spins! The grace is there,
But strain as well is plain to see.
Degas loved the two together:
Beauty joined to energy.

Edgar Degas purchased once
A fine El Greco, which he kept
Against the wall beside his bed
To hang his pants on while he slept.

ODE TO PLEASURE

from the French of La Fontaine

PLEASURE, whom had we lacked from earliest hour,
To live or die had come to seem as one,
Of all creatures the sole magnet-stone,
How surely are we drawn by thy great power!
 Here, thou art mover of all things.
 For thee, for thy soft blandishings
 We fly to troubles and to harms.
 No captain is, nor man-at-arms,
Nor subject, minister, nor royalty,
 Who does not singly aim at thee.
We other nurslings, did not our labors bear
The fruits of fame, delicious to the ear,
And were this sound not pleasurably heard,
 Then should we rhyme a single word?
That which the world calls glory, and acclaims,
Which served as guerdon in the Olympic games,
Truly is none but thee, O divine Pleasure.
And shall the joys of sense not fill thy measure?
 For whom are Flora's gifts outlaid,
 The Sunset and Aurora made,
 Pomona and her tasty fare,
 Bacchus, soul of banquets rare,
 Waters, and forest-lands, and leas,
 The nourishers of reveries?
Wherefore so many arts, thy children all?
Why all these Chlorises, whose charms enthrall,
 Unless to make thy commerce thrive?
My meaning's innocent: whatever limit
 Rigor may for desire contrive,
 Nevertheless there's pleasure in it.

O Pleasure, Pleasure, in the former age
     Mistress of Hellas' gayest sage,
Pray scorn me not, come thence and stop with me;
     Idle thou shalt never be:
For games I love, and love, and every art,
Country, and town, and all; there's nought my mood
     May not convert to sovereign good,
Even to the gloom of melancholy heart.
Then come; and wouldst thou know, O sweetest Pleasure,
What measure of these goods must me befall?
Enough to fill a hundred years of leisure;
     For thirty were no good at all.

Haze, char, and the weather of All Souls':
A giant absence mopes upon the trees:
Leaves cast in casual potpourris
Whisper their scents from pits and cellar-holes.

Or brewed in gulleys, steeped in wells, they spend
In chilly steam their last aromas, yield
From shallow hells a revenance of field
And orchard air. And now the envious mind

Which could not hold the summer in my head
While bounded by that blazing circumstance
Parades these barrens in a golden trance,
Remembering the wealthy season dead,

And by an autumn inspiration makes
A summer all its own. Green boughs arise
Through all the boundless backward of the eyes,
And the soul bathes in warm conceptual lakes.

Less proud than this, my body leans an ear
Past cold and colder weather after wings'
Soft commotion, the sudden race of springs,
The goddess' tread heard on the dayward stair,

Longs for the brush of the freighted air, for smells
Of grass and cordial lilac, for the sight
Of green leaves building into the light
And azure water hoisting out of wells.

MARCHÉ AUX OISEAUX

Hundreds of birds are singing in the square.
Their minor voices fountaining in air
And constant as a fountain, lightly loud,
Do not drown out the burden of the crowd.

Far from his gold Sudan, the travailleur
Lends to the noise an intermittent chirr
Which to his hearers seems more joy than rage.
He batters softly at his wooden cage.

Here are the silver-bill, the orange-cheek,
The perroquet, the dainty coral-beak
Stacked in their cages; and around them move
The buyers in their termless hunt for love.

Here are the old, the ill, the imperial child;
The lonely people, desperate and mild;
The ugly; past these faces one can read
The tyranny of one outrageous need.

We love the small, said Burke. And if the small
Be not yet small enough, why then by Hell
We'll cramp it till it knows but how to feed,
And we'll provide the water and the seed.

JUGGLER

A ball will bounce, but less and less. It's not
A light-hearted thing, resents its own resilience.
Falling is what it loves, and the earth falls
So in our hearts from brilliance,
Settles and is forgot.
It takes a sky-blue juggler with five red balls

To shake our gravity up. Whee, in the air
The balls roll round, wheel on his wheeling hands,
Learning the ways of lightness, alter to spheres
Grazing his finger ends,
Cling to their courses there,
Swinging a small heaven about his ears.

But a heaven is easier made of nothing at all
Than the earth regained, and still and sole within
The spin of worlds, with a gesture sure and noble
He reels that heaven in,
Landing it ball by ball,
And trades it all for a broom, a plate, a table.

Oh, on his toe the table is turning, the broom's
Balancing up on his nose, and the plate whirls
On the tip of the broom! Damn, what a show, we cry:
The boys stamp, and the girls
Shriek, and the drum booms
And all comes down, and he bows and says good-bye.

If the juggler is tired now, if the broom stands
In the dust again, if the table starts to drop
Through the daily dark again, and though the plate
Lies flat on the table top,
For him we batter our hands
Who has won for once over the world's weight.

PARABLE

I read how Quixote in his random ride
Came to a crossing once, and lest he lose
The purity of chance, would not decide

Whither to fare, but wished his horse to choose.
For glory lay wherever he might turn.
His head was light with pride, his horse's shoes

Were heavy, and he headed for the barn.

Its piers less black for sunny smiles above,
My roadstead hand takes all the world for sea,
Or lifts to wingèd love
Its limed and leafless tree,
Or creeps into a glove
To greet mine enemy.

Angers the noble face
Would suffer unexpressed
This lackey in his place
Must serve to manifest,
Be mailed without as any carapace,
But soft within, where self to self is pressed.

Nights, when the head to other glory sets,
The hand turns turtle, lying like a lake
Where men with broken nets
Seek, for their master's sake,
All that that lord forgets
Because he would not wake.

Above the ceded plains
Visored volition stands
And sees my lands in chains
And ponders the commands
Of what were not impossible campaigns
If I would take my life into my hands.

PITY

The following day was overcast, each street
A slow canal to float him to the place
Where he'd let fall the dear and staring face,
A funnel toward the thin reproachful tweet.

All day the starved canary called him back
In newsboy's whistle, crying of a tire,
Squeak of a squeegee, sirens finding fire,
Until the nightfall packed his head in black,

And he went back and climbed the stairs again,
Stepping across her body, freed the bird,
Which left its cage and out the window whirred
As a bad thought out of a cracked brain.

THE SIRENS

I never knew the road
From which the whole earth didn't call away,
With wild birds rounding the hill crowns,
Haling out of the heart an old dismay,
Or the shore somewhere pounding its slow code,
Or low-lighted towns
Seeming to tell me, stay.

Lands I have never seen
And shall not see, loves I will not forget,
All I have missed, or slighted, or foregone
Call to me now. And weaken me. And yet
I would not walk a road without a scene.
I listen going on,
The richer for regret.

Now winter downs the dying of the year,
And night is all a settlement of snow;
From the soft street the rooms of houses show
A gathered light, a shapen atmosphere,
Like frozen-over lakes whose ice is thin
And still allows some stirring down within.

I've known the wind by water banks to shake
The late leaves down, which frozen where they fell
And held in ice as dancers in a spell
Fluttered all winter long into a lake;
Graved on the dark in gestures of descent,
They seemed their own most perfect monument.

There was perfection in the death of ferns
Which laid their fragile cheeks against the stone
A million years. Great mammoths overthrown
Composedly have made their long sojourns,
Like palaces of patience, in the gray
And changeless lands of ice. And at Pompeii

The little dog lay curled and did not rise
But slept the deeper as the ashes rose
And found the people incomplete, and froze
The random hands, the loose unready eyes
Of men expecting yet another sun
To do the shapely thing they had not done.

These sudden ends of time must give us pause.
We fray into the future, rarely wrought
Save in the tapestries of afterthought.
More time, more time. Barrages of applause
Come muffled from a buried radio.
The New-year bells are wrangling with the snow.

Sidling upon the river, the white boat
Has volleyed with its cannon all the morning,
Shaken the shore towns like a Judgment warning,
Telling the palsied water its demand
That the crime come to the top again, and float,
That the sunk murder rise to the light and land.

Blam. In the noon's perfected brilliance burn
Brief blooms of flame, which soil away in smoke;
And down below, where slowed concussion broke
The umber stroll of waters, water-dust
Dreamily powders up, and serves to turn
The river surface to a cloudy rust.

Down from his bridge the river captain cries
To fire again. They make the cannon sound;
But none of them would wish the murder found,
Nor wish in other manner to atone
Than booming at their midnight crime, which lies
Rotting the river, weighted with a stone.

GRASSE: THE OLIVE TREES

for Marcelle and Ferdinand Springer

Here luxury's the common lot. The light
Lies on the rain-pocked rocks like yellow wool
And around the rocks the soil is rusty bright
From too much wealth of water, so that the grass
Mashes under the foot, and all is full
Of heat and juice and a heavy jammed excess.

Whatever moves moves with the slow complete
Gestures of statuary. Flower smells
Are set in the golden day, and shelled in heat,
Pine and columnar cypress stand. The palm
Sinks its combs in the sky. This whole South swells
To a soft rigor, a rich and crowded calm.

Only the olive contradicts. My eye,
Traveling slopes of rust and green, arrests
And rests from plenitude where olives lie
Like clouds of doubt against the earth's array.
Their faint disheveled foliage divests
The sunlight of its color and its sway.

Not that the olive spurns the sun; its leaves
Scatter and point to every part of the sky,
Like famished fingers waving. Brilliance weaves
And sombers down among them, and among
The anxious silver branches, down to the dry
And twisted trunk, by rooted hunger wrung.

Even when seen from near, the olive shows
A hue of far away. Perhaps for this
The dove brought olive back, a tree which grows
Unearthly pale, which ever dims and dries,
And whose great thirst, exceeding all excess,
Teaches the South it is not paradise.

THE AVOWAL

from the French of Villiers de l'Isle Adam

I have lost the wood, the heath,
Fresh Aprils long gone by. . . .
Give me your lips: their breath
Shall be the forest's sigh.

I have lost the sullen Sea,
Its glooms, its echoed caves;
Speak only: it shall be
The murmur of the waves.

By royal grief oppressed
I dream of a vanished light. . . .
Hold me: in that pale breast
Shall be the calm of night.

THE GIFTS

from the French of Villiers de l'Isle Adam

If you speak to me, some night,
Of my sick heart's secret bale,
To ease you I'll recite
An ancient ballad-tale.

Or if you speak of pain
And hopes long fallen due,
I shall but gather then
The dew-filled rose for you.

If, like the flower which grows
In the exile soil of graves,
You beg to share my woes . . .
I'll bring you a gift of doves.

When night believes itself alone
It is most natural, conceals
No artifice. The open moon
With webs in sky and water wields

The slightest wave. This vision yields
To a cool accord of semblance, land
Leasing each wave the palest peals
Of bright apparent notes of sand.

The bathers whitely come and stand.
Water diffuses them, their hair
Like seaweed slurs the shoulders, and
Their voices in the moonstrung air

Go plucked of words. Now wading where
The moon's misprision salves them in-
To silver, they are unaware
How lost they are when they begin

To mix with water, making then
Gestures of blithe obedience,
As five Danilovas within
The soft compulsions of their dance.

THE TERRACE

De la vaporisation et de la centralisation du Moi. Tout est là.
BAUDELAIRE

We ate with steeps of sky about our shoulders,
High up a mountainside,
On a terrace like a raft roving
Seas of view.

The tablecloth was green, and blurred away
Toward verdure far and wide,
And all the country came to be
Our table too.

We drank in tilted glasses of rosé
From tinted peaks of snow,
Tasting the frothy mist, and freshest
Fathoms of air.

Women were washing linens in a stream
Deep down below,
The sound of water over their knuckles
A sauce rare.

Imminent towns whose weatherbeaten walls
Looked like the finest cheese
Bowled us enormous melons from their
Tolling towers.

Mixt into all the day we heard the spice
Of many tangy bees
Eddying through the miles-deep
Salad of flowers.

When we were done we had our hunger still;
We dipped our cups in light;

We caught the fine-spun shade of clouds
In spoon and plate;

Drunk with imagined breathing, we inhaled
The dancing smell of height;
We fished for the bark of a dog, the squeak
Of a pasture gate.

But for all our benedictions and our gay
Readily said graces,
The evening stole our provender and
Left us there,

And darkness filled the specious space, and fell
Betwixt our silent faces,
Pressing against our eyes its absent
Fathomless stare.

Out in the dark we felt the real mountains
Hulking in proper might,
And we felt the edge of the black wind's
Regardless cleave,

And we knew we had eaten not the manna of heaven
But our own reflected light,
And we were the only part of the night that we
Couldn't believe.

A PROBLEM FROM MILTON

In Eden palm and open-handed pine
Displayed to God and man their flat perfection.
Carefully coiled, the regulation vine
Submitted to our general sire's inspection.

And yet the streams in mazy error went;
Powdery flowers a potent odor gave;
The trees, on second thoughts, were lushly blent
And swashed forever like a piling wave.

The builded comber like a hurdling horse
Achieves the rocks. With wild informal roar
The spray upholds its freedom and its force,
But leaves the limpet and the whelk ashore.

In spirals of the whelk's eternal shell
The mind of Swedenborg to heaven flew,
But found it such a mathematic hell
That Emerson was damned if it would do.

Poor Adam, deviled by your energy,
What power egged you on to feed your brains?
Envy the gorgeous gallops of the sea,
Whose horses never know their lunar reins.

A GLANCE FROM THE BRIDGE

Letting the eye descend from reeking stack
And black façade to where the river goes,
You see the freeze has started in to crack
(As if the city squeezed it in a vice),
And here and there the limbering water shows,
And gulls colonial on the sullied ice.

Some rise and braid their glidings, white and spare,
Or sweep the hemmed-in river up and down,
Making a litheness in the barriered air,
And through the town the freshening water swirls
As if an ancient whore undid her gown
And showed a body almost like a girl's.

CLEARNESS

There is a poignancy in all things clear,
In the stare of the deer, in the ring of a hammer in the morning.
Seeing a bucket of perfectly lucid water
We fall to imagining prodigious honesties.

And feel so when the snow for all its softness
Tumbles in adamant forms, turning and turning
Its perfect faces, littering on our sight
The heirs and types of timeless dynasties.

In pine-woods once that huge precision of leaves
Amazed my eyes and closed them down a dream.
I lost to mind the usual southern river,
Mud, mist, the plushy sound of the oar,

And pondering north through lifted veils of gulls,
Through sharpening calls, and blue clearings of steam,
I came and anchored by a fabulous town
Immaculate, high, and never found before.

This was the town of my mind's exacted vision
Where truths fell from the bells like a jackpot of dimes,
And the people's voices, carrying over the water,
Sang in the ear as clear and sweet as birds.

But this was Thulë of the mind's worst vanity;
Nor could I tell the burden of those clear chimes;
And the fog fell, and the stainless voices faded;
I had not understood their lovely words.

*

The asterisk
Says look below, as a star
We prize for its being far
And longing ask
For some release,
Joins to a dog or a bear,
A dipper, a tipping chair.
They give us peace
These downward looks
Of stars, the way they note
The birth of gods, and dote
On seaward brooks.
Some of the sea's
Stars are alive, I've seen
Them figure the white-green
Ocean frieze;
And I've known
The sea so rich and black
It gave the starlight back
Brighter. It shone
As if the high
Vault were its glass, and thus
It is. It's up to us
To gloss the sky.

:

From barren coldness birds
Go squadroned South;
So from the hollow mouth
The way of words
Is East. When written down
As here, they file
In broken bands awhile,
But never noun
Found what it named; for lame,
Lost, though they burn
For the East, all words must turn
Back where they came
From, back to their old
Capital. Still,
As pilgrims on a hill
Fallen, behold
With failing eyes from far
The desired city,
Silence will take pity
On words. There are
Pauses where words must wait,
Spaces in speech
Which stop and calm it, and each
Is like a gate:

Past which creation lies
In morning sun,
Where word with world is one
And nothing dies.

The land was overmuch like scenery,
The flowers attentive, the grass too garrulous green;
In the lake like a dropped kerchief could be seen
The lark's reflection after the lark was gone;
The Roman road lay paved too shiningly
For a road so many men had traveled on.

Also the people were strange, were strangely warm.
The king recalled the father of his guest,
The queen brought mead in a studded cup, the rest
Were kind, but in all was a vagueness and a strain,
Because they lived in a land of daily harm.
And they said the same things again and again.

It was a childish country; and a child,
Grown monstrous, so besieged them in the night
That all their daytimes were a dream of fright
That it would come and own them to the bone.
The hero, to his battle reconciled,
Promised to meet that monster all alone.

So then the people wandered to their sleep
And left him standing in the echoed hall.
They heard the rafters rattle fit to fall,
The child departing with a broken groan,
And found their champion in a rest so deep
His head lay harder sealed than any stone.

The land was overmuch like scenery,
The lake gave up the lark, but now its song
Fell to no ear, the flowers too were wrong,
The day was fresh and pale and swiftly old,

The night put out no smiles upon the sea;
And the people were strange, the people strangely cold.

They gave him horse and harness, helmet and mail,
A jeweled shield, an ancient battle-sword,
Such gifts as are the hero's hard reward
And bid him do again what he has done.
These things he stowed beneath his parting sail,
And wept that he could share them with no son.

He died in his own country a kinless king,
A name heavy with deeds, and mourned as one
Will mourn for the frozen year when it is done.
They buried him next the sea on a thrust of land:
Twelve men rode round his barrow all in a ring,
Singing of him what they could understand.

Still, citizen sparrow, this vulture which you call
Unnatural, let him but lumber again to air
Over the rotten office, let him bear
The carrion ballast up, and at the tall

Tip of the sky lie cruising. Then you'll see
That no more beautiful bird is in heaven's height,
No wider more placid wings, no watchfuller flight;
He shoulders nature there, the frightfully free,

The naked-headed one. Pardon him, you
Who dart in the orchard aisles, for it is he
Devours death, mocks mutability,
Has heart to make an end, keeps nature new.

Thinking of Noah, childheart, try to forget
How for so many bedlam hours his saw
Soured the song of birds with its wheezy gnaw,
And the slam of his hammer all the day beset

The people's ears. Forget that he could bear
To see the towns like coral under the keel,
And the fields so dismal deep. Try rather to feel
How high and weary it was, on the waters where

He rocked his only world, and everyone's.
Forgive the hero, you who would have died
Gladly with all you knew; he rode that tide
To Ararat; all men are Noah's sons.

WELLFLEET: THE HOUSE

Roof overwoven by a soft tussle of leaves,
The walls awave with sumac shadow, lilac
Lofts and falls in the yard, and the house believes
It's guarded, garlanded in a former while.

Here one cannot intrude, the stillness being
Lichenlike grown, a coating of quietudes;
The portraits dream themselves, they are done with seeing;
Rocker and teacart balance in iron moods.

Yet for the transient here is no offense,
Because at certain hours a wallowed light
Floods at the seaside windows, vague, intense,
And lays on all within a mending blight,

Making the kitchen silver blindly gleam,
The yellow floorboards swim, the dazzled clock
Boom with a buoy sound, the chambers seem
Alluvial as that champed and glittering rock

The sea strokes up to fashion dune and beach
In strew by strew, and year by hundred years.
One is at home here. Nowhere in ocean's reach
Can time have any foreignness or fears.

THE DEATH OF A TOAD

A toad the power mower caught,
Chewed and clipped of a leg, with a hobbling hop has got
  To the garden verge, and sanctuaried him
  Under the cineraria leaves, in the shade
    Of the ashen heartshaped leaves, in a dim,
      Low, and a final glade.

The rare original heartsblood goes,
Spends on the earthen hide, in the folds and wizenings, flows
  In the gutters of the banked and staring eyes. He lies
  As still as if he would return to stone,
    And soundlessly attending, dies
      Toward some deep monotone,

Toward misted and ebullient seas
And cooling shores, toward lost Amphibia's emperies.
  Day dwindles, drowning, and at length is gone
  In the wide and antique eyes, which still appear
    To watch, across the castrate lawn,
      The haggard daylight steer.

DRIFTWOOD

In greenwoods once these relics must have known
A rapt, gradual growing,
That are cast here like slag of the old
Engine of grief;

Must have affirmed in annual increase
Their close selves, knowing
Their own nature only, and that
Bringing to leaf.

Say, for the seven cities or a war
Their solitude was taken,
They into masts shaven, or milled into
Oar and plank;

Afterward sailing long and to lost ends,
By groundless water shaken,
Well they availed their vessels till they
Smashed or sank.

Then on the great generality of waters
Floated their singleness,
And in all that deep subsumption they were
Never dissolved;

But shaped and flowingly fretted by the waves'
Ever surpassing stress,
With the gnarled swerve and tangle of tides
Finely involved.

Brought in the end where breakers dump and slew
On the glass verge of the land,

Silver they rang to the stones when the sea
Flung them and turned.

Curious crowns and scepters they look to me
Here on the gold sand,
Warped, wry, but having the beauty of
Excellence earned.

In a time of continual dry abdications
And of damp complicities,
They are fit to be taken for signs, these emblems
Royally sane,

Which have ridden to homeless wreck, and long revolved
In the lathe of all the seas,
But have saved in spite of it all their dense
Ingenerate grain.

A COURTYARD THAW

The sun was strong enough today
To climb the wall and loose the courtyard trees
(For two short hours, anyway)
From hardship of the January freeze.

Their icy cerements decayed
To silken moistures, which began to slip
In glints and spangles down, and made
On every twig a bauble at the tip.

No blossom, leaf or basking fruit
Showed ever such pure passion for the sun
As these cold drops that knew no root
Yet filled with light and swelled and one by one

(Or showered by a wingbeat, sown
From windbent branches in arpeggios)
Let go and took their shinings down
And brought their brittle season to a close.

O false gemmation! Flashy fall!
The eye is pleased when nature stoops to art,
Staging within a courtyard wall
Such twinkling scenes. But puzzling to the heart,

This spring was neither fierce nor gay;
This summary autumn fell without a tear:
No tinkling music-box can play
The slow, deep-grounded masses of the year.

LAMENT

Nashe's old queens who bartered young and fair
Their light tiaras for such ponderous stones:
Of them I'd think, how sunlit still their hair,
And fine as airship frames their balanced bones.

It is, I say, a most material loss.
Kept spirit is corporate; doubly the thought of you.
As air fills air, or waves together toss,
Out of my wishes and your being grew.

Water and air: such unclenched stuff can last,
But rarest things are visible and firm;
Grace falls the fastest from our failing past,
And I lament for grace's early term,

For casual dances that your body knows,
Whose spirit only sense can understand,
For times when spirit, doomed and single, flows
Into the speeches of your eye and hand.

FLUMEN TENEBRARUM

This night's colossal quiet, in heaven crowned
Immoveable, at earth is slippered swift
With shore grasses' wind-ushering sound,
With the river's folding drift,

With our own vanishing voices as we go
By the stream side, watching our shadows dangled
Down the bank to the flood, trailed in the flow
And all in stars entangled.

There is the hunter hulking up the night
Who waded once the wildest of our seas,
With foiled eyes marking the still flight
Of the faint Pleiades.

And here are we, who hold each other now
So nearly, that our welded shadows seem,
There where they fall away, a ghostly prow
Steering into the stream.

As if to kiss were someway to embark;
As if to love were partly to be spent,
And send of us a hostage to the dark.
If so, I am content,

And would not have my lively longing freeze,
Nor your delays, in figures of the sky,
Since none outlasts the stream, and even these
Must come to life and die.

The hunter shall be tumbled in this tide,
Worse stricken than by Dian's steepest arrow,

And all his fire shall gutter out beside
This old embarcadero;

Those nymphs, so long preserved, at last be lost,
Be borne again along this blackening race,
And with their lover swept away, and tossed
In scintillant embrace.

FROM THE LOOKOUT ROCK

Oh wind I hear you faltering,
In long cessation dying down,
Failing the osprey's pillowed wing,
Franchising all the peaceful graves,
The lifted waters letting fall
And all the flags of every town,
Because your slackened voices crawl
To bass finales in their caves.

The parching stones along the shore
Hastily sip the listless waves,
In doubt the sea will pour them more
When lull has loitered into calm;
A tenantry of jays in swarm
Issues rebellious from the leaves
And rising makes a patch of storm
Above the quiet of their elm.

Good-bye the roving of the land:
The tumbling weed of all the West
Engraves its shadow on the sand.
Haphazard stand the weather-vanes,
Unrocked the cradles of the vales,
The ropes are loose of every mast,
Appalled are all the sagging sails
And overhushed the ocean-lanes.

The fishers for Atlantis see
A stillness on the ocean grow
Deeper than that of history.
Venturers to the pole turn round
And watch the southward cities fill
With space as barren as their snow.

The cities' voices fall and still
To hear the wide retreat of sound.

I from this rock espy a gull
Riding the raveled last of air
Who folds his wings, and tips to fall
Beside the pillar of the sun.
(The drumhead bay is like a lake,
A great and waiting skyward stare.)
The shoreline gives a timbrel shake:
Our last Icarian moment, done.

Gods of the wind, return again,
For this was not the peace we prayed;
Intone again your burdened strain,
And weave the world to harmony,
Voyage the seed along the breeze,
Reviving all your former trade,
Restore the lilting of the trees
And massive dances of the sea.

TO AN AMERICAN POET JUST DEAD

In the *Boston Sunday Herald* just three lines
Of no-point type for you who used to sing
The praises of imaginary wines,
And died, or so I'm told, of the real thing.

Also gone, but a lot less forgotten,
Are an eminent cut-rate druggist, a lover of Giving,
A lender, and various brokers: gone from this rotten
Taxable world to a higher standard of living.

It is out in the comfy suburbs I read you are dead,
And the soupy summer is settling, full of the yawns
Of Sunday fathers loitering late in bed,
And the ssshh of sprays on all the little lawns.

Will the sprays weep wide for you their chaplet tears?
For you will the deep-freeze units melt and mourn?
For you will Studebakers shred their gears
And sound from each garage a muted horn?

They won't. In summer sunk and stupefied
The suburbs deepen in their sleep of death.
And though they sleep the sounder since you died
It's just as well that now you save your breath.

GIACOMETTI

Rock insults us, hard and so boldly browed
Its scorn needs not to focus, and with fists
Which still unstirring strike:
Collected it resists
Until its buried glare begets a like
Anger in us, and finds our hardness. Proud,

Then, and armed, and with a patient rage
We carve cliff, shear stone to blocks,
And down to the image of man
Batter and shape the rock's
Fierce composure, closing its veins within
That outside man, itself its captive cage.

So we can baffle rock, and in our will
Can clothe and keep it. But if our will, though locked
In stone it clutches, change,
Then are we much worse mocked
Than cliffs can do: then we ourselves are strange
To what we were, which lowers on us still.

High in the air those habitants of stone
Look heavenward, lean to a thought, or stride
Toward some concluded war,
While we on every side,
Random as shells the sea drops down ashore,
Are walking, walking, many and alone.

What stony shape could hold us now, what hard
Bent can we bulk in air, where shall our feet
Come to a common stand?
Follow along this street

(Where rock recovers carven eye and hand),
Open the gate, and cross the narrow yard

And look where Giacometti in a room
Dim as a cave of the sea, has built the man
We are, and made him walk:
Towering like a thin
Coral, out of a reef of plaster chalk,
This is the single form we can assume.

We are this man unspeakably alone
Yet stripped of the singular utterly, shaved and scraped
Of all but being there,
Whose fullness is escaped
Like a burst balloon's: no nakedness so bare
As flesh gone in inquiring of the bone.

He is pruned of every gesture, saving only
The habit of coming and going. Every pace
Shuffles a million feet.
The faces in this face
Are all forgotten faces of the street
Gathered to one anonymous and lonely.

No prince and no Leviathan, he is made
Of infinite farewells. Oh never more
Diminished, nonetheless
Embodied here, we are
This starless walker, one who cannot guess
His will, his keel his nose's bony blade.

And volumes hover round like future shades
This least of man, in whom we join and take

A pilgrim's step behind,
And in whose guise we make
Our grim departures now, walking to find
What railleries of rock, what palisades?

HE WAS

a brown old man with a green thumb:
I can remember the screak on stones of his hoe,
The chug, choke, and high madrigal wheeze
Of the spray-cart bumping below
The sputtery leaves of the apple trees,
But he was all but dumb

Who filled some quarter of the day with sound
All of my childhood long. For all I heard
Of all his labors, I can now recall
Never a single word
Until he went in the dead of fall
To the drowsy underground,

Having planted a young orchard with so great care
In that last year that none was lost, and May
Aroused them all, the leaves saying the land's
Praise for the livening clay,
And the found voice of his buried hands
Rose in the sparrowy air.

A SIMILE FOR HER SMILE

Your smiling, or the hope, the thought of it,
Makes in my mind such pause and abrupt ease
As when the highway bridgegates fall,
Balking the hasty traffic, which must sit
On each side massed and staring, while
Deliberately the drawbridge starts to rise:

Then horns are hushed, the oilsmoke rarefies,
Above the idling motors one can tell
The packet's smooth approach, the slip,
Slip of the silken river past the sides,
The ringing of clear bells, the dip
And slow cascading of the paddle wheel.

CEREMONY

A striped blouse in a clearing by Bazille
Is, you may say, a patroness of boughs
Too queenly kind toward nature to be kin.
But ceremony never did conceal,
Save to the silly eye, which all allows,
How much we are the woods we wander in.

Let her be some Sabrina fresh from stream,
Lucent as shallows slowed by wading sun,
Bedded on fern, the flowers' cynosure:
Then nymph and wood must nod and strive to dream
That she is airy earth, the trees, undone,
Must ape her languor natural and pure.

Ho-hum. I am for wit and wakefulness,
And love this feigning lady by Bazille.
What's lightly hid is deepest understood,
And when with social smile and formal dress
She teaches leaves to curtsey and quadrille,
I think there are most tigers in the wood.

The Beautiful Changes
and Other Poems

1947

FOR CHARLEE

CIGALES

You know those windless summer evenings, swollen to stasis
by too-substantial melodies, rich as a
running-down record, ground round
to full quiet. Even the leaves
have thick tongues.

And if the first crickets quicken then,
other inhabitants, at window or door
or rising from table, feel in the lungs
a slim false-freshness, by this
trick of the ear.

Chanters of miracles took for a simple sign
the Latin cigale, because of his long waiting
and sweet change in daylight, and his singing
all his life, pinched on the ash leaf,
heedless of ants.

Others made morals; all were puzzled and joyed
by this gratuitous song. Such a plain thing
morals could not surround, nor listening:
not "chirr" nor "cri-cri." There is no straight
way of approaching it.

This thin uncomprehended song it is
springs healing questions into binding air.
Fabre, by firing all the municipal cannon
under a piping tree, found out
cigales cannot hear.

There was an infidel who
Walked past all churches crying,
Yet wouldn't have changed his tears,
Not for the smoothest-worn pew;
You've seen
Caddis flies walking on spring-surface, water walkers who breathe
Air and know water, with weakly wings
Drying to pelt and sheen;

There is something they mean

By breaking from water and flying
Lightly some hours in air,
Then to the water-top dropping,
Floating their heirs and dying:
It's like
Paulsaul the Jew born in Tarshish, who when at bay on the steps
With Hebrew intrigued those Jewsotted Jews
Crowding to stone and strike;

Always alike and unlike,

Walking the point where air
Mists into water, and knowing
Both, with his breath, to be real,
Roman he went everywhere:
I've been
Down in Virginia at night, I remember an evening door
A table lamp lit; light stretched on the lawn,
Seeming to ask me in;

I thought if I should begin

To enter entirely that door,
Saying, "I am a son of this house,

My birth and my love are here,"
I might never come forth any more:
Air mists
Into water, past odors of halls and the fade of familial voices,
Stair creaks, piano tones falling on rugs,
Wallpaper palimpsests:

Armored the larva rests

Dreaming the streambottom tides,
Writhing at times to respire, and
Sealing to him flat stones,
He closely abides, abides:
One night
I sat till dawn on a porch, rocked in a cane-bottom chair,
In Geneseo, in Illinois,
Rocking from light to light;

Silent and out of sight

I saw the houses sleep
And the autos beside them sleeping,
The neat plots, the like trustful houses,
Minute, armoreal, deep;
Wind went
Tamely and samely as puppies, tousling the Japanese maples,
Lawnsprays and tricycles waited for sun,
Shyly things said what they meant:

An old man stitching a tent

Could have been Saul in Tharsos,
Loved and revered; instead
He carried Jew visions to Greeks
For adoration or curses;
For he
Troubled them; whether they called him "babbler" or hailed him
"Mercurios"

(Scarcely restrained from killing him oxen),
His wasn't light company:

Still pearled with water, to be

Ravished by air makes him grow
Stranger to both, and discover
Heaven and hell in the poise
Betwixt "inhabit" and "know";
I hold
Here in my head Maine's bit speech, lithe laughter of Mobile blacks,
Opinions of salesmen, ripe tones of priests,
Plaints of the bought and sold:

Can I rest and observe unfold

The imminent singletax state,
The Negro rebellion, the rise
Of the nudist cult, the return
Of the Habsburgs, watch and wait
And praise
The spirit and not the cause, and neatly precipitate
What is not doctrine, what is not bound
To enclosured ground; what stays?

Lives that the caddis fly lays

Twixt air and water, must lie
Long under water—how Saul
Cursed once the market babblers,
Righteous could watch them die!
Who learns
How hid the trick is of justice, cannot go home, nor can leave,
But the dilemma, cherished, tyrannical,
While he despairs and burns

Da capo da capo returns.

TYWATER

Death of Sir Nihil, book the *nth*,
Upon the charred and clotted sward,
Lacking the lily of our Lord,
Alases of the hyacinth.

Could flicker from behind his ear
A whistling silver throwing knife
And with a holler punch the life
Out of a swallow in the air.

Behind the lariat's butterfly
Shuttled his white and gritted grin,
And cuts of sky would roll within
The noose-hole, when he spun it high.

The violent, neat and practiced skill
Was all he loved and all he learned;
When he was hit, his body turned
To clumsy dirt before it fell.

And what to say of him, God knows.
Such violence. And such repose.

They have gone into the gray hills quilled with birches,
Drag now their cannon up the chill mountains;
But it's going to be long before
Their war's gone for good.

I tell you it hits at childhood more than churches
Full up with sky or buried town fountains,
Rooms laid open or anything
Cut stone or cut wood,

Seeing the boys come swinging slow over the grass
(Like playing pendulum) their silver plates,
Stepping with care and listening
Hard for hid metal's cry.

It's rightly-called-chaste Belphoebe some would miss,
Some, calendar colts at Kentucky gates;
But the remotest would guess that
Some scheme's gone awry.

Danger is sunk in the pastures, the woods are sly,
Ingenuity's covered with flowers!
We thought woods were wise but never
Implicated, never involved.

Cows in mid-munch go splattered over the sky;
Roses like brush-whores smile from bowers;
Shepherds must learn a new language; this
Isn't going to be quickly solved.

Sunshiny field grass, the woods floor, are so mixed up
With earliest trusts, you have to pick back
Far past all you have learned, to go
Disinherit the dumb child,

Tell him to trust things alike and never to stop
Emptying things, but not let them lack
Love in some manner restored; to be
Sure the whole world's wild.

POTATO

for André du Bouchet

An underground grower, blind and a common brown;
Got a misshapen look, it's nudged where it could;
Simple as soil yet crowded as earth with all.

Cut open raw, it looses a cool clean stench,
Mineral acid seeping from pores of prest meal;
It is like breaching a strangely refreshing tomb:

Therein the taste of first stones, the hands of dead slaves,
Waters men drank in the earliest frightful woods,
Flint chips, and peat, and the cinders of buried camps.

Scrubbed under faucet water the planet skin
Polishes yellow, but tears to the plain insides;
Parching, the white's blue-hearted like hungry hands.

All of the cold dark kitchens, and war-frozen gray
Evening at window; I remember so many
Peeling potatoes quietly into chipt pails.

"It was potatoes saved us, they kept us alive."
Then they had something to say akin to praise
For the mean earth-apples, too common to cherish or steal.

Times being hard, the Sikh and the Senegalese,
Hobo and Okie, the body of Jesus the Jew,
Vestigial virtues, are eaten; we shall survive.

What has not lost its savor shall hold us up,
And we are praising what saves us, what fills the need.
(Soon there'll be packets again, with Algerian fruits.)

Oh, it will not bear polish, the ancient potato,
Needn't be nourished by Caesars, will blow anywhere,
Hidden by nature, counted-on, stubborn and blind.

You may have noticed the bush that it pushes to air,
Comical-delicate, sometimes with second-rate flowers
Awkward and milky and beautiful only to hunger.

FIRST SNOW IN ALSACE

The snow came down last night like moths
Burned on the moon; it fell till dawn,
Covered the town with simple cloths.

Absolute snow lies rumpled on
What shellbursts scattered and deranged,
Entangled railings, crevassed lawn.

As if it did not know they'd changed,
Snow smoothly clasps the roofs of homes
Fear-gutted, trustless and estranged.

The ration stacks are milky domes;
Across the ammunition pile
The snow has climbed in sparkling combs.

You think: beyond the town a mile
Or two, this snowfall fills the eyes
Of soldiers dead a little while.

Persons and persons in disguise,
Walking the new air white and fine,
Trade glances quick with shared surprise.

At children's windows, heaped, benign,
As always, winter shines the most,
And frost makes marvelous designs.

The night guard coming from his post,
Ten first-snows back in thought, walks slow
And warms him with a boyish boast:

He was the first to see the snow.

ON THE EYES OF AN SS OFFICER

I think of Amundsen, enormously bit
By arch-dark flurries on the ice plateaus,
An amorist of violent virgin snows
At the cold end of the world's spit.

Or a Bombay saint asquat in the market place,
Eyes gone from staring the sun over the sky,
Who still dead-reckons that acetylene eye,
An eclipsed mind in a blind face.

But this one's iced or ashen eyes devise,
Foul purities, in flesh their wilderness,
Their fire; I ask my makeshift God of this
My opulent bric-a-brac earth to damn his eyes.

Now homing tradesmen scatter through the streets
Toward suppers, thinking on improved conditions,
While evening, with a million simple fissions,
Takes up its warehouse watches, storefront beats,
By nursery windows its assigned positions.

Now at the corners of the Place Pigalle
Bright bars explode against the dark's embraces;
The soldiers come, the boys with ancient faces,
Seeking their ancient friends, who stroll and loll
Amid the glares and glass: electric graces.

The puppies are asleep, and snore the hounds;
But here wry hares, the soldier and the whore,
Mark off their refuge with a gaudy door,
Brazen at bay, and boldly out of bounds:
The puppies dream, the hounds superbly snore.

Ionized innocence: this pair reclines,
She on the table, he in a tilting chair,
With Arden ease; her eyes as pale as air
Travel his priestgoat face; his hand's thick tines
Touch the gold whorls of her Corinthian hair.

"Girl, if I love thee not, then let me die;
Do I not scorn to change my state with kings?
Your muchtouched flesh, incalculable, which wrings
Me so, now shall I gently seize in my
Desperate soldier's hands which kill all things."

VIOLET AND JASPER

Outside, the heirs of purity pick by,
Pecked by petite damnations, sweatless still
Along the burning marle of Cambridge; here
The light that spanks the windows takes a spill
Over the lint-bright curtain to the floor
Or frays through glasses, curly as a vine.

Broad Violet, her lettuce head all full
Of bawdry and novenas, yanks the tap,
Carries a beer to Jasper where he dreams
Of lucky numbers, falls upon his lap:
Her wandy fingers paddling on his dome
Trouble the face of El Dorado's pool.

Rumors of plenty flutter these around,
Riot, mercy and treasure haven here,
In silly brains monastically kept,
In Cambridge, where I homing saw appear
In a pharmacy window-globe ruddily rapt
Suddenly streaming with blood this turnip town.

THE PEACE OF CITIES

Terrible streets, the manichee hell of twilight
Glides like a giant bass between your windows,

Dark deploying in minnows into your alleys
Stirs and hushes the reefs of scudding trash.

Withinwalls voices, past the ports and locks,
Murmur below the shifting of crockery

I know not what; the barriered day expires
In scattered sounds of dread inconsequence.

Ah, this is no andante, there will come
No primavera, there was a louder and deeper

Peace in those other cities, when silver fear
Drove the people to fields, and there they heard

The Luftwaffe waft what let the sunshine in
And blew the bolt from everybody's door.

THE GIAOUR AND THE PACHA
(Eugène Delacroix, 1856)

The Pacha sank at last upon his knee
And saw his ancient enemy reared high
In mica dust upon a horse of bronze,
The sun carousing in his either eye,

Which of a sudden clouds, and lifts away
The light of day, of triumph; and the scene
Takes tenderly the one already dead
With secret hands of strong and bitter green.

As secretly, the cloak becomes aware
Of floating, mane and tail turn tracery;
Imbedded in the air, the Giaour stares
And feels the pistol fall beside his knee.

"Is this my anger, and is this the end
Of gaudy sword and jeweled harness, joy
In strength and heat and swiftness, that I must
Now bend, and with a slaughtering shot destroy

The counterpoise of all my force and pride?
These falling hills and piteous mists; O sky,
Come loose the light of fury on this height,
That I may end the chase, and ask not why."

UP, JACK

Prince Harry turns from Percy's pouring sides,
Full of the kind of death that honor makes
By pouring all the man into an act;
So simplified by battle, he mistakes

A hibernating Jack for dead Sir John.
"Poor pumpkin, I am cold since you are done,
For if you proved but yellow pulp within,
You were this nature's kindest earthly sun."

Exit the Prince; now Jack will rise again,
No larger now, nor spun of stuff more fine,
And only to his feet, and yet a god
To our short summer days and the world's wine.

Up, Jack! For Percy sinks in darker red,
And those who walk away are dying men.
Great Falstaff (*rising*) clears his thirsty throat,
And I'm content, and Hal is hale again.

IN A BIRD SANCTUARY

Because they could not give it too much ground
they closely planted it with fir and shrub.
A plan of pathways, voted by the Club,
contrived to lead the respiter around
a mildly wandring wood, still at no cost
to get him lost.

Now over dear Miss Drury's favored trees
they flutter (birds) and either stop or not,
as if they were unconscious that the spot
is planned for them, and meant to buy release
for one restrained department of the soul,
to "make men whole."

It's hard to tell the purpose of a bird;
for relevance it does not seem to try.
No line can trace no flute exemplify
its traveling; it darts without the word.
Who wills devoutly to absorb, contain,
birds give him pain.

Commissoners of Public Parks have won
a partial wisdom, know that birds exist.
And seeing people equally insist
on birds and statues, they go hire a man
to swab sans rancor dung from granite stare
and marble hair.

BIRDS HAVE BEEN SEEN IN TOWERS AND ON ISLES;
ALSO ON PRIVY TOPS, IN FANEUIL HALL;
BIRDS HAVE SOME OF THEM NOT BEEN SEEN AT ALL;
BIRDS, IF THEY CARE TO, WALK ALONG IN FILE.
BIRDS DO NOT FEEL ESPECIALLY GOOD IN FLIGHT:
LET'S TREAT THEM RIGHT!

The liberty of any things becomes
the liberty of all. It also brings
their abolition into anythings.
In order's name let's not turn down our thumbs
on routine visions; we must figure out
what all's about.

JUNE LIGHT

Your voice, with clear location of June days,
Called me—outside the window. You were there,
Light yet composed, as in the just soft stare
Of uncontested summer all things raise
Plainly their seeming into seamless air.

Then your love looked as simple and entire
As that picked pear you tossed me, and your face
As legible as pearskin's fleck and trace,
Which promise always wine, by mottled fire
More fatal fleshed than ever human grace.

And your gay gift—Oh when I saw it fall
Into my hands, through all that naïve light,
It seemed as blessed with truth and new delight
As must have been the first great gift of all.

A SONG

As at the bottom of a seething well
A phosphorus girl is singing,
Up whispering galleries trellised notes
Climb and cling.

It is a summer-song an old man wrote
Out of the winter's wringing,
He hunched in a cold room, back to frost's
Sledge and sting.

Desperate, gentle, every phrase declines
As fruit to groundward weighs,
As all things seek their shadows, yearn,
Yearn and fall.

She may be singing Iowa afternoons,
Lightshifting corn ballets,
Scattering stutter of windmills, each throat's
Very clear call;

Nevertheless, the balconies are in tune
And all but a single child
Are hushed in sweet relinquishing, in
Praise of time.

But the white child is puzzled, cannot hear,
To loss not reconciled
Has heartroom still for sorrows, needs no
Song or rhyme.

THE WALGH-VOGEL

More pleasurable to look than feed upon,
Hence unconserved in dodo-runs, the round,
Unfeathered, melancholy, more than fifty pound
Dodo is gone,

Who when incarnate wore two token wings
And dined on rocks, to mock at mockeries.
Empowered now by absence, blessed with tireless ease,
It soars and sings

Elated in our skies, wherever seen.
Absolute retractility allows
Its wings be wavy wide as heaven; silence endows
Its hoots serene

With airy spleenlessness all may unhear.
Alive the dodo strove for lack of point,
Extinct won superfluity, and can disjoint
To joy our fear.

Dive, dodo, on the earth you left forlorn,
Sit vastly on the branches of our trees,
And chant us grandly all improbabilities.

Our uncrowned kings have no such regal rind
As this; their purple stain
Is in the mind.
God was more kind to this wronged kingly fruit
And pedigreed it plain.
It makes no suit

For rule in gardens, yields to the Brussels sprout,
Knows that the scornful sun
Will seek it out
In exile, and so blazon in its sheen
That it may cow and stun
Turnip and bean.

Natural pomp! Excessive Nightshades' Prince!
Polished potato, you wear
An Egyptian rinse
Of Belladonna's hues, a crown that's green,
And do not have the care
Of storing spleen,

Because your purple presence is reproof!
Before God gave him rue
And raised the roof,
Unoriginal Adam, bloat with cant
Celestial, christened you
The *Egg*-plant.

OBJECTS

Meridians are a net
Which catches nothing; that sea-scampering bird
The gull, though shores lapse every side from sight, can yet
Sense him to land, but Hanno had not heard

Hesperidean song,
Had he not gone by watchful periploi:
Chalk rocks, and isles like beasts, and mountain stains along
The water-hem, calmed him at last near-by

The clear high hidden chant
Blown from the spellbound coast, where under drifts
Of sunlight, under plated leaves, they guard the plant
By praising it. Among the wedding gifts

Of Herë, were a set
Of golden McIntoshes, from the Greek
Imagination. Guard and gild what's common, and forget
Uses and prices and names; have objects speak.

There's classic and there's quaint,
And then there is that devout intransitive eye
Of Pieter de Hooch: see feinting from his plot of paint
The trench of light on boards, the much-mended dry

Courtyard wall of brick,
And sun submerged in beer, and streaming in glasses,
The weave of a sleeve, the careful and undulant tile. A quick
Change of the eye and all this calmly passes

Into a day, into magic.
For is there any end to true textures, to true
Integuments; do they ever desist from tacit, tragic
Fading away? Oh maculate, cracked, askew,

Gay-pocked and potsherd world
I voyage, where in every tangible tree
I see afloat among the leaves, all calm and curled,
The Cheshire smile which sets me fearfully free.

A DUTCH COURTYARD

What wholly blameless fun
To stand and look at pictures. Ah, they are
Immune to us. This courtyard may appear
To be consumed with sun,

Most mortally to burn,
Yet it is quite beyond the reach of eyes
Or thoughts, this place and moment oxidize;
This girl will never turn,

Cry what you dare, but smiles
Tirelessly toward the seated cavalier,
Who will not proffer you his pot of beer;
And your most lavish wiles

Can never turn this chair
To proper uses, nor your guile evict
These tenants. What surprising strict
Propriety! In despair,

Consumed with greedy ire,
Old Andrew Mellon glowered at this Dutch
Courtyard, until it bothered him so much
He bought the thing entire.

A smoky rain riddles the ocean plains,
Rings on the beaches' stones, stomps in the swales,
Batters the panes
Of the shore hotel, and the hoped-for summer chills and fails.
The summer people sigh,
"Is this July?"

They talk by the lobby fire but no one hears
For the thrum of the rain. In the dim and sounding halls,
Din at the ears,
Dark at the eyes well in the head, and the ping-pong balls
Scatter their hollow knocks
Like crazy clocks.

But up in his room by artificial light
My father paints the summer, and his brush
Tricks into sight
The prosperous sleep, the girdling stir and clear steep hush
Of a summer never seen,
A granted green.

Summer, luxuriant Sahara, the orchard spray
Gales in the Eden trees, the knight again
Can cast away
His burning mail, Rome is at Anzio: but the rain
For the ping-pong's optative bop
Will never stop.

Caught Summer is always an imagined time.
Time gave it, yes, but time out of any mind.
There must be prime
In the heart to beget that season, to reach past rain and find
Riding the palest days
Its perfect blaze.

FOLK TUNE

When Bunyan swung his whopping axe
The forests strummed as one loud lute,
The timber crashed beside his foot
And sprung up stretching in his tracks.

He had an ox, but his was blue.
The flower in his buttonhole
Was brighter than a parasol.
He's gone. Tom Swift has vanished too,

Who worked at none but wit's expense,
Putting dirigibles together
Out in the yard, in the quiet weather,
Whistling behind Tom Sawyer's fence.

Now when the darkness in my street
Nibbles the last and crusty crumbs
Of sound, and all the city numbs
And goes to sleep upon its feet,

I listen hard to hear its dreams:
John Henry is our nightmare friend,
Whose shoulders roll without an end,
Whose veins pump, pump and burst their seams,

Whose sledge is smashing at the rock
And makes the sickly city toss
And half awake in sighs of loss
Until the screaming of the clock.

John Henry's hammer and his will
Are here and ringing out our wrong,
I hear him driving all night long
To beat the leisured snarling drill

SUN AND AIR

The air staggers under the sun, and heat-morasses
Flutter the birds down; wind barely climbs the hills,
Saws thin and splinters among the roots of the grasses;

All stir sickens, and falls into barn shadows, spills
Into hot hay and heat-hammered road dust, makes no sound,
Waiting the sun's siege out to collect its wills.

As a hound stretched sleeping will all on a sudden bound,
Air will arise all sinews, crack-crying, tear tether,
Plow sheets of powder high, heave sky from milling ground.

So sun and air, when these two goods war together,
Who else can tune day's face to a softest laugh,
Being sweet beat the world with a most wild weather,

Trample with light or blow all heaven blind with chaff.

TWO SONGS IN A STANZA OF BEDDOES·

I

That lavished sunlight, where
And lilac-mottled air,
And where the fair-skinned winds
 That touched the plum
To fall? All gone; my mind's
Lost all the summer, binds
 No beauty home.

How have such seas of sun
Cast me so dry here? Run,
Mindseye, and find a field
 Embered with clover . . .
Why is my heart congealed,
All the sweet season sealed
 Off from her lover?

Stretch, tamarack, and strain;
Lash, poplar; and complain,
Guttering grasses; seek
 For summer, swallow:
And mind, fill full of creak
And hustling scraps, be bleak
 And howling-hollow.

Come tender winter, weep
This raving earth to sleep;
Your deadly tears disguise
 In lightest white.
Frost these forgetful eyes
From day's sheet-metal skies
 And viselike night.

II

Through tossing views, the gull,
All-balancing, can scull
The sky, and strew its calls
 On the breeze;
Its shivered shadow crawls
The leisured azure brawls
 Of the seas.

When then from day's blue brink
Its rapt reflections sink,
A bird made dark, unclear,
 To sea-deep flies,
And monstrous flutters there,
And slow and loud with fear
 Cries and cries.

THE WATERS

From powdery Palmyre, the tireless wind,
Braided by waves but cradling to this shore,
Where folding water leaves Atlantis' gold,
Dust of Aurelian's sack, scrawls in the sand,
Streams in the salty grass the stainless cries
Of fighters at the gate, and strews the trees
With, milled by many days, Zenobia's priceless robe.

And the sunned wind, as the wave thins and slips
Into rock-pools, lies in the shallows of the spine.
And the mind, as the sand rises and rolls in the pull
Of the wave, yields to the cry of the buried child.

The sea so sings us back to histories
On every perilous beach. At Juan-les-Pins
Or Coney Isle, the bathers lie between
Yellow and blue, in the handling of such soft air
That real caresses leaf the thinnest hair,
Maternal murmurs sweep the dozing head;
And gazing out from underneath our arms,
We see the spring of feet from brightened sand;
We feel the world lie warm beneath the hand;
And hear the cry of voices over water,
Or horns of vessels very far from land.

And only the dull are safe, only the dead
Are safe from the limitless swell and the bitter seethe,
The sea's lumbering sigh that says it carries
So many stars and suns, and yet will wreathe
A rock with webs of foam and maidenhair.
Von Aschenbach, when he perceived the fair
Aureate child before the endless sea,
Shingled his painted face in agony.

For the damnedest lovers of water dread the waves:
The inland painters in whose canvases
We read some vaporized and fierce devotion
To "the smiling of women, and the motion
Of great waters"; the pauper poet who dreamed
Of sunken rivers, yet who scorned to seek
Their sources in the caves of the world; and he
Who mad and weak, became a sailingcraft
On heilignüchterne lakes of memory.

SUPERIORITIES

Malachy stamped the diving decks
And shouted to the frigging wind
"Frig on!," and hove an empty quart
Into the stomach of a wave.

Phipps at the bucking rail was still
And keenly modest as a star,
Attentive to each blast and surge,
And so becalmed the storm in him.

How far superior to those
Huddled below with wives and buddies,
Comforting, caring, sharing pills,
Prayers and other proper studies.

A SIMPLIFICATION

Those great rough ranters, Branns
And catarrhal Colonels, who hurled
Terrible taunts at the vault, ripped down Jesus' banns
And widowed the world

With Inquisitorial thunder, dammed-
Up Biblical damnations, were
The last with tongues to topple heaven; they hammed
Jahweh away and here

We are. The decorous god
Simply withdrew. If you hear
A good round rhetoric anywhere give me the nod.
I'd like to hear

Bryan lying and quoting sic
Transit nux vomica. These foetal-
Voiced people lack eloquence to blow a sick
Maggot off a dead beetle.

A DUBIOUS NIGHT

A bell diphthonging in an atmosphere
Of shying night air summons some to prayer
Down in the town, two deep lone miles from here,

Yet wallows faint or sudden everywhere,
In every ear, as if the twist wind wrung
Some ten years' tangled echoes from the air.

What kyries it says are mauled among
The queer elisions of the mist and murk,
Of lights and shapes; the senses were unstrung,

Except that one star's synecdochic smirk
Burns steadily to me, that nothing's odd
And firm as ever is the masterwork.

I weary of the confidence of God.

L'ETOILE
(Degas, 1876)

A rushing music, seizing on her dance,
Now lifts it from her, blind into the light;
And blind the dancer, tiptoe on the boards
Reaches a moment toward her dance's flight.

Even as she aspires in loudening shine
The music pales and sweetens, sinks away;
And past her arabesque in shadow show
The fixt feet of the maître de ballet.

So she will turn and walk through metal halls
To where some ancient woman will unmesh
Her small strict shape, and yawns will turn her face
Into a little wilderness of flesh.

SUNLIGHT IS IMAGINATION

Each shift you make in the sunlight somewhere
Cleaves you away into dark. Now
You are clarion hair, bright brow,
Lightcaped shoulder and armside here, and there
Gone into meadow shadow. Where
Are my eyes to run?
Shall I say you are fair
In the sun,
Or mermaid you in the grass waving away?

Shall I say
    The whole green day builds hither to lift
    This flare of your hair?, I wielding such sight
    As did Juan Ponce, climbing to light
    On a morning of the Feast of the Resurrection. Aloft
    On the ocean shelf he saw the soft
    Signals of trees
    And gulls, and the sift
    Of the sea's
    Long landward airs offering trails to him.

And dim
    Each flower of Florida, but all
    Was shining; parrots prophesied;
    Vines ciphered; to each waterside
    Paths pitched in hopes to the fair and noble well
    Of sweetest savor and reflaire
    Whose ghostly taste
    And cleanse repair
    All waste,
    And where was ageless power from the first.

Yet thirst
    Makes deserts, barrens to a sign
    Deckled and delicate arbors, bleeds
    The rose, parches the prodigal seeds
    That spring toward time in air, and breaks the spine
    Of the rock. No; I shall resign
    That power, and crave
    Kindly to pine
    And to save
    The sprout and the ponderation of the land.

My hand
    Can touch but mysteries, and each
    Of a special shadow. I shall spare
    The larch its shattering ghost, the pear
    Its dark awaiter too, for shades beseech
    Originals: they running reach
    On windy days
    To touch, to teach
    What stays
    Is changed, and shadows die into dying things.

Now swings
    The sky to noon, and mysteries run
    To cover; let our love not blight
    The various world, but trust the flight
    Of love that falls again where it begun.
    All creatures are, and are undone.
    Then lose them, lose
    With love each one,
    And choose
    To welcome love in the lively wasting sun.

A slopeshouldered shape from scurrying burdens
Backward and forth, or perhaps a lyre
Or a clef wrung wry in tuning untunable tones,
Or a knot for tugging an out-of-hand

Vine to the trellis in clerical gardens:
Sweetness & light, ice & fire,
Nature & art have dissocketed all your bones,
Porter, poor pander ampersand.

O

The idle dayseye, the laborious wheel,
The osprey's tours, the pointblank matin sun
Sanctified first the circle; thence for fun
Doctors deduced a shape, which some called real
(So all games spoil), a shape of spare appeal,
Cryptic and clean, and endlessly spinning unspun.
Now I go backward, filling by one and one
Circles with hickory spokes and rich soft shields
Of petalled dayseyes, with herehastening steel
Volleys of daylight, writhing white looks of sun;
And I toss circles skyward to be undone
By actual wings, for wanting this repeal
I should go whirling a thin Euclidean reel,
No hawk or hickory to true my run.

THE REGATTA

A rowdy wind pushed out the sky,
Now swoops the lake and booms in sails;
Sunlight can plummet, when it fails,
Brighten on boats which pitch and fly.

Out on the dock-end, Mrs. Vane,
Seated with friends, lifts lenses to
Delighted eyes, and sweeps the view
Of "galleons" on the "raging main."

A heeling boat invades the glass
To turn a buoy; figures duck
The crossing sail—"There's Midge and Buck!
I know his scarf!"—the sailors pass.

The hotel guests make joking bets,
And Mrs. Vane has turned, inquired
If Mr. Vane is feeling "tired."
He means to answer, but forgets.

She offers him binoculars:
A swift, light thing is slipping on
The bitter waters, always gone
Before the wave can make it hers;

So simply it evades, evades,
So weightless and immune may go,
The free thing does not need to know
How deep the waters are with shades.

It's but a trick; and still one feels
Franchised a little—God knows I
Would be the last alive to cry
To Whatzisname, "I love thy wheels!"

Freedom's a pattern. I am cold.
I don't know what I'm doing here.
And Mrs. Vane says, "Home now, dear."
He rises, does as he is told;
Hugging her arm, he climbs the pier.
Behind him breaks the triumph cheer.

BELL SPEECH

The selfsame toothless voice for death or bridal:
It has been long since men would give the time
To tell each someone's-change with a special chime,
And a toll for every year the dead walked through.
And mostly now, above this urgent idle
Town, the bells mark time, as they can do.

This bavardage of early and of late
Is what is wanted, and yet the bells beseech
By some excess that's in their stricken speech
Less meanly to be heard. Were this not so,
Why should Great Paul shake every window plate
To warn me that my pocket watch is slow?

Whether or not attended, bells will chant
With a clear dumb sound, and wide of any word
Expound our hours, clear as the waves are heard
Crashing at Mount Desert, from far at sea,
And dumbly joining, as the night's descent
Makes deltas into dark of every tree.

Great Paul, great pail of sound, still dip and draw
Dark speech from the deep and quiet steeple well,
Bring dark for doctrine, do but dim and quell
All voice in yours, while earth will give you breath.
Still gather to a language without flaw
Our loves, and all the hours of our death.

Poplar, absolute danseuse,
Wind-wed and faithless to wind, troweling air
Tinily everywhere faster than air can fill,
Here whitely rising, there
Winding, there
Feinting to earth with a greener spill,
Never be still, whose pure mobility
Can hold up crowding heaven with a tree.

Sycamore, trawled by the tilt sun,
Still scrawl your trunk with tattered lights, and keep
The spotted toad upon your patchy bark,
Baffle the sight to sleep,
Be such a deep
Rapids of lacing light and dark,
My eye will never know the dry disease
Of thinking things no more than what he sees.

A script of trees before the hill
Spells cold, with laden serifs; all the walls
Are battlemented still;
But winter spring is winnowing the air
Of chill, and crawls
Wet-sparkling on the gutters;
Everywhere
Walls wince, and there's the steal of waters.

Now all this proud royaume
Is Veniced. Through the drift's mined dome
One sees the rowdy rusted grass,
And we're amazed as windows stricken bright.
This too-soon spring will pass
Perhaps tonight,
And doubtless it is dangerous to love
This somersault of seasons;
But I am weary of
The winter way of loving things for reasons.

The kingdom of air, of lightly looming air
That crowns us all king spinners, let it swing
Wide of the earth and any foundering
In the sea's reflection, the forest's manifold snare.

Air is refreshment's treasury; earth seems
Our history's faulted sink, and spring of love;
And we between these dreamt-of empires move
To coop infinity away from dreams.

See, every yard, alive with laundry white,
Billowing wives and leaves, gives way to air:
A blown pedestrian upon the square
Tosses a clanging trolley out of sight.

Then air relents to skyward with a sigh,
Earth's adamant variety is remade;
The hanging dust above the streets is staid
And solid as the walls of Central High.

Contagions of the solid make this day
An infiniteness any eye may prove.
Let asphalt bear us up to walk in love,
Electric towers shore the clouds away.

GRACE

" 'The young lambs bound As to the tabor's
sound.' They toss and toss; it is as if it were the
earth that flung them, not themselves. It is
the pitch of graceful agility when we think that."

G. M. HOPKINS, Notebooks

So active they seem passive, little sheep
Please, and Nijinsky's out-the-window leap
And marvelous midair pause please too
A taste for blithe brute reflex; flesh made word
Is grace's revenue.

One is tickled, again, by the dining-car waiter's absurd
Acrobacy—tipfingered tray like a wind-besting bird
Plumblines his swinging shoes, the sole things sure
In the shaken train; but this is all done for food,
Is habitude, if not pure

Hebetude. It is a graph of a theme that flings
The dancer kneeling on nothing into the wings,
And Nijinsky hadn't the words to make the laws
For learning to loiter in air; he "merely" said,
"I merely leap and pause."

Lambs are constrained to bound. Consider instead
The intricate neural grace in Hamlet's head;
A grace not barbarous implies a choice
Of courses, not in a lingo of leaps-in-air
But in such a waiting voice·

As one would expect to hear in the talk of Flaubert,
Piety makes for awkwardness, and where
Balance is not urgent, what one utters
May be puzzled and perfect, and we respect
Some scholars' stutters.

Even fraction-of-a-second action is not wrecked
By a graceful still reserve. To be unchecked
Is needful then: choose, challenge, jump, poise, run. . .
Nevertheless, the praiseful, graceful soldier
Shouldn't be fired by his gun.

A birdsnest built on the palm of the high-
Most bough of an elm, this morning as I came by
A brute gust lifted-and-left in the midst of the air;
 Whereat the leaves went quiet, and there
 Was a moment of silence in honor of
The sweetness of danger. The chalice now bobbing above,
Of interlaid daintiest timber, began the chute
 Down forty fell feet toward stone and root
 With a drift and a sampan spin, and gripped
Loosely its fineshelled life; now viciously tipped
By a ripple of air, with an acrobat's quick not-quite-
 Lost, dipped lower to whirl upright;
 Then, with a straight-down settling, it
Descended into sunshine, and, with a hushed touch, lit
On a mesa of strenuous grass. Oh risk-hallowed eggs, oh
 Triumph of lightness! Legerity begs no
 Quarter: my Aunt Virginia, when
She'd relapsed and recovered, would sit in the garden again
Waiting, all lapped in an indigo-flowered shawl,
 In white for her "regular customers'" call;
 Whose pity she parried with very-blue-eyed
Attention, and giggled and patted their hands when they tried
To do-something-for-her; she sat in the heart of her days
 And watched with a look of peculiar praise;
 Her slight voice could catch a pleasure complete
As a gull takes a fish at the flash of his side. Her great
Heavy husband adored her, would treat with a sudden blind sally
 Of softness his "visitor from the valley";
 He called her "Birdie," which was good, for him.
And he and the others, the strong, the involved, in-the-swim,
Seeing her there in the garden, in her gay shroud
 As vague and as self-possessed as a cloud,
 Requiring nothing of them any more,
And one hand lightly laid on a fatal door,
Thought of the health of the sick, and, what mocked their sighing,
 Of the strange intactness of the gladly dying.

FOR ELLEN

On eyes embarked for sleep the only light
Goes off, and there is nothing that you know
So well, it may not monster in this sea.
The vine leaves pat the screen. Viciously free,
The wind vaults over the roof with Mister Crow
To drop his crooked laughter in your night.

And morning's cannonades of brightness come
To a little utter blueness in your eyes.
You stagger goldenly, bestowing blue;
Blue heal-all breaks the pavingstone where you
Expect it, and you laugh in pure surprise
At the comic cripple hurdling to his slum.

But sometime you will look at the lazy sun
Hammocked in clouds, dead-slumbering in the sky.
That casual fire will blister blue, and night
Will strand its fears; then with a starker sight
And newer darker love, you will supply
The world of joy which never was begun.

CASERTA GARDEN

Their garden has a silent tall stone-wall
So overburst with drowsing trees and vines
None but a stranger would remark at all
The barrier within the fractured lines.

I doubt they know it's there, or what it's for—
To keep the sun-impasted road apart,
The beggar, soldier, renegade and whore,
The dust, the sweating ox, the screeching cart.

They'd say, "But this is how a garden's made":
To fall through days in silence dark and cool,
And hear the fountain falling in the shade
Tell changeless time upon the garden pool.

See from the tiptoe boy—the dolphin throats—
The fine spray bending; jets collapse in rings
Into the round pool, and each circle floats
Wide to the verge, and fails in shimmerings.

A childhood by this fountain wondering
Would leave impress of circle-mysteries:
One would have faith that the unjustest thing
Had geometric grace past what one sees.

How beauties will grow richer walled about!
This tortile trunk, old paradigm of pain,
These cherished flowers—they dream and look not out,
And seem to have no need of earth or rain.

In heavy peace, walled out necessity,
How devious the lavish grapevine crawls,
And trails its shade, irrelevant and free,
In delicate cedillas on the walls.

And still without, the dusty shouting way,
Hills lazar-skinned, with hungry-rooted trees,
And towns of men, below a staring day,
Go scattered to the turning mountain frieze.

The garden of the world, which no one sees,
Never had walls, is fugitive with lives;
Its shapes escape our simpler symmetries;
There is no resting where it rots and thrives.

PRAISE IN SUMMER

Obscurely yet most surely called to praise,
As sometimes summer calls us all, I said
The hills are heavens full of branching ways
Where star-nosed moles fly overhead the dead;
I said the trees are mines in air, I said
See how the sparrow burrows in the sky!
And then I wondered why this mad *instead*
Perverts our praise to uncreation, why
Such savor's in this wrenching things awry.
Does sense so stale that it must needs derange
The world to know it? To a praiseful eye
Should it not be enough of fresh and strange
That trees grow green, and moles can course in clay,
And sparrows sweep the ceiling of our day?

THE BEAUTIFUL CHANGES

One wading a Fall meadow finds on all sides
The Queen Anne's Lace lying like lilies
On water; it glides
So from the walker, it turns
Dry grass to a lake, as the slightest shade of you
Valleys my mind in fabulous blue Lucernes.

The beautiful changes as a forest is changed
By a chameleon's tuning his skin to it;
As a mantis, arranged
On a green leaf, grows
Into it, makes the leaf leafier, and proves
Any greenness is deeper than anyone knows.

Your hands hold roses always in a way that says
They are not only yours; the beautiful changes
In such kind ways,
Wishing ever to sunder
Things and things' selves for a second finding, to lose
For a moment all that it touches back to wonder.

NOTES

MINED COUNTRY: *Silver Plates:* mine detectors.

UP, JACK: *King Henry IV, Part I,* Act V, Scene 4.

THE WALGH-VOGEL: Title and first stanza derived from Sir Thomas Herbert's *Travels,* quoted in Phipson's *Animal-Lore of Shakspeare's Time.*

OBJECTS: *A Dutch Courtyard,* by Pieter de Hooch, is in the National Gallery at Washington.

THE WATERS: The last section refers to Leonardo via Walter Pater, Villiers de l'Isle Adam, and Holderlin. These artists, particularly the two last, seem to me to have suffered similar emotional tragedies.

A SIMPLIFICATION: Brann the iconoclast was shot dead on the streets of Waco in 1898. Not an important figure, but his name has the irascible sound I was seeking.